George W. Gue

Our Country's Flag

George W. Gue

Our Country's Flag

ISBN/EAN: 9783337100827

Printed in Europe, USA, Canada, Australia, Japan

Cover: Foto ©ninafisch / pixelio.de

More available books at **www.hansebooks.com**

One Country and One Flag.

OUR COUNTRY'S FLAG

—:⋄⦂⋄:——

REV. GEORGE W. GUE

PASTOR FIRST METHODIST

Late Chaplain 108th Reg. Ills. Volunteers

AND

Chaplain Dep't

:⋄⦂⋄:

ILLUSTRATED

Copyright, January, 1890,
By G. W. Gue.

Recopyright, November, 1890.

OUR LOVELY BANN[ER]

Ne'er waved beneath the golden s[un]
    A lovelier banner for the bra[ve]
Than that our bleeding fathers wo[n]
    And proudly to their children [gave]
Nor earth a fairer gem can bring[ ]
    Or freedom claim a brighter s[ ]
Than that to which our free heart[s]
    The flag which lights the fre[e]

This Souvenir

Is most respectfully dedicated to all who love Our Country's Flag, and are in sympathy with the institutions which it represents.

THE AUTHOR.

CONTENTS.

	Page
Introduction,	1
Rev. Charles W. Ayling.	
Preface,	5
Rev. George W. Gue.	
Acknowledgment,	7
Rev. George W. Gue.	
The History of Our Country's Flag,	10
Rev. Addis Albro, LL. B., D. D.	
Birthplace of the American Flag,	16
Charles J. Budd.	
Desecration of the Flag,	19
Anonymous.	
Magnifying the Flag,	20
Anonymous.	
Our Country's Flag,	22
Rev. A. D. Perrin, M. A.	
Daniel Webster on "Our Flag,"	24
Our National Banner,	25
William Dexter Smith.	
The Number and Order of Stars in Our Country's Flag.	26

	Page
Our Flag,	27
Anonymous.	
Freedom's Flag,	28
Henry Ward Beecher.	
The American Flag,	29
Joseph Rodman Drake.	
Our Country's Flag—When Adopted by Congress,	31
Fifteen Stripes and Fifteen Stars,	32
The Soldier's Pride,	33
R. Tompkins.	
What the Flag Means to Comrades,	34
John F. Chase.	
Swing Out the Flag.	35
J. W. Kingon.	
Henry Ward Beecher on the American Flag,	37
God Bless Our Flag,	39
J. C. O. Redington.	
Stand Up for the Flag,	40
Mrs. M. S. Kidder.	
The Flag of the United States,	41
Lizzie T. Gassett.	
The Flag's Birthday,	43
Mary A. P. Stansbury.	
Crown-Prince of Germany and the United States Flag,	46

I Love Thee, Dear Banner,	47
Rev. George W. Gue.	
Flag of the Noble,	48
William Freeman.	
The Beautiful Flag of the Free,	49
Anonymous.	
Our Flag on the Andes Mountains,	50
The Old Flag,	51
Miss Minnie G. McArthur.	
How to Construct Our Flag,	53
The Stars and Stripes of Old,	55
C. Jay.	
Raise the Star-Gemmed Banner,	56
Adelaide George Bennett.	
The Fort McHenry Flag Exhibited in 1876,	57
Hail Our Flag,	58
Harry C. Burns.	
Flag of Our Union Forever,	59
George P. Morris.	
There are Two Things Holy,	60
Victor Hugo.	
Columbia's Flag,	61
William Dinsmore.	
Unfurl the Glorious Banner,	63
Anonymous.	

	Page.
The National Ensign.	64
Robert C. Winthrop.	
The Stripes and the Stars,	65
Edna Dean Proctor.	
Stand by the Old Flag,	67
Robert M. Wilson.	
The Star-Spangled Banner.	69
Francis Scott Key.	
The Author of the Star-Spangled Banner,	71
Rally 'Round the Old Flag,	73
Comrade Redington.	
Forever Float the Old Flag,	74
J. C. O. Redington.	
Our Flag of the Free.	75
Anonymous.	
Rally 'Round Your Country's Flag,	76
Stephen A. Douglass.	
Our Flag,	77
Ninette M. Lowater.	
Keep the Flag in View,	78
Anonymous.	
The First United States Flag Around the World,	79
Our Flag in the South,	80
C. C. Baylor.	
Lieutenant-General Winfield Scott and the United States Flag,	81

		Page
Our Flag of Liberty,	.	82
Colonel S. D. Richardson.		
The First United States Flag in the Interior of China,		84
The United States Flag at the Completion of the Union Pacific Railroad,		85
One Flag Only,	. . .	86
General Daniel E. Sickles.		
Our Glorious Flag, .	. .	87
H. C. Ballard.		
The Flag Our Hero Bore,	.	88
I. J. Bielby.		
Hail to Our Banner,	. .	89
W. P. Tilden.		
Our Star-Gemmed Banner — Spirit of 1861.		90
H. E. T.		
Our Country's Flag on God's Sacred Altars, .	.	93
J. W. Temple.		
Proudly in Glory Floating O'er Us,		94
J. E. Thorp.		
Conference Resolution Regarding Our Country's Flag,		95
Our Flag and the Cross, .	.	96
Colonel Hepburn.		
The Flag O'er Our School-House is Floating,		97
J. C. O. Redington.		
Our Flag in the School-Room,	.	98
Hon. Andrew S. Draper.		

xiv

	Page.
Our Glorious Ensign, . . Anonymous.	99
The Flag Over Our Churches. . Rev. E. A. Anderson.	100
The Stars and Stripes, . Anonymous.	101
Stand by the Flag, . . . J. C. O. Redington.	103
Our Star-Spangled Emblem, . J. C. O. Redington.	104
Our Flag and the Union Forever. . Rev. J. Matlock.	105
Tell the Glad Tidings, . . Anonymous.	106
Blessings on Our Banner. . J. C. O. Redington.	107
The Meaning of Our Flag. . Colonel R. G. Ingersoll.	108
Let Our Flag Float Over Each. Anonymous.	109
The United States Flag at North Cape, Norway,	110
Keep the Flag at the Front, . . J. C. O. Redington.	111
Wrap the Flag Around Me, Boys, . P. Stewart Taylor.	112

	Page
Hurrah for the Flag, . . .	113
Miss M. H. Howliston.	
Hurrah for the Old Flag.	114
Anonymous.	
The Children's Song of the Flag,	115
Anonymous.	
Preferred Death to Surrendering the Flag.	116
The American Flag in Our Schools,	117
J. C. O. Redington.	
The Flag of the Constellation,	119
T. Buchanan Read.	
The American Flag in Nashville, Tennessee.	120
Oh, Wrap Me in the Flag. .	122
Comrade Chaplain E. Dennison.	
Let Us Have Peace, . . .	124
General R. A. Alger.	
The Flag's Come Back to Tennessee.	125
No Desecration of "Old Glory,"	127
Our Banner of Glory, . . .	128
J. C. O. Redington.	
A Lovely Banner,	130
Anonymous.	
The National Flag, . . .	131
Hon. Charles Sumner.	
Colors that Will not Run,	132

Our Country's Flag in the White House.

Flag of Glory, . . .
      J. D. Phelps.

My Father's Flag and Mine. .
      Rev. J. H. Lozier.

Sons of Veterans and Our Flag,
      Colonel J. H. Pierce.

The Patriot's Flag, . .
      Newton Bateman.

Our Banner, . . .
      David Paul Brown.

The Glorious Ensign, . .
      Anonymous.

Our Banner of Light,
      J. C. S.

The United States Flag in Battle,

Our Honored Flag, . .
      James W. Temple.

James A. Garfield and Our Flag. .

Our Glorious Flag, . . .
      Hon. Edward J. Preston.

Flag of My Country, . .
      William Parsons Lunt.

Dedication of a United States Flag Sent by Ladies of New York to the Seventh Regiment.
      Anonymous.

	Page.
Our Flag is There,	149
A Naval Officer.	
The Flag Restored,	150
E Pluribus Unum,	151
George Washington Cutter.	
A Lesson to be Taught in Our Public Schools,	154
Dr. Richard Edwards.	
Our Flag, Our Pride,	155
J. C. O. Redington.	
The Flag of Sumter and Final Union,	156
Anonymous.	
A Flag of 1776 at the Centennial, 1876,	157
The Hallowed Flag,	158
Professor J. Howard Wert.	
Brave Words,	160
Colonel James Mulligan.	
The Flag With Forty-Two Stars,	161
J. C. O. Redington.	
Extract from Hon. Edward Everett's Eloquent Speech at a Flag-Raising in Boston, 1861,	162
Flag of Yankee Doodle,	164
Anonymous.	
Saved by Singing the Star-Spangled Banner,	165
The Banner of the Union,	166
Kate Brownlee Sherwood.	

	Page.
Italians Honoring Our Flag,	167
The Heraldry of the American Flag,	168
Charles J. Lukens.	
The Colors in Our Flag—What they Represent,	170
Freedom's Flag.	171
Giebel.	
The Flag and the Union,	172
Rufus Choate.	
The First Union Flag Over the Capitol of the Confederacy After the Surrender,	173
Our Star-Spangled Banner Forever,	174
Nellie Griswold Johnson.	
Money Bequeathed for Flags,	175
All One Under the Stars and Stripes,	177
Anonymous.	
A Monopoly of the Flag,	178
Yes, Our Flag is Still Advancing,	179
Chaplain Lozier.	
Stand by Our Country's Flag,	181
Anonymous.	
The Beauties of the American Flag,	182
George F. Hoar.	
Our Grand Old Flag,	183
J. P. Martin.	
A Memorable Command,	184
John A. Dix.	

xix

	Page
Our Country's Flag in Switzerland,	185
Our Battle-Flags, . .	186
Moses G. Owen.	
The Nation's Firm Bulwark — The Sons of Veterans,	187
Charles F. Griffin.	
Gov. Yates and the American Flag,	189
Under the Flag of Our Fathers, .	190
George H. Boker.	
Rally 'Round Our Flag, . . .	191
James T. Fields.	
Hymn to the Flag, . . .	192
Comrade E. W. Foster.	
The Tattered Banner, .	193
Anonymous.	
Old Glory, . . .	194
A. Read Wales.	
The Flag of the Sixth Indiana,	195
Return of the Flags to Their States,	196
Alfred B. Street.	
Our Banner on the Soldier's Bier, .	197
Our Flag and the Soldier's Grave, .	199
Anonymous.	
Wrapt in Our Flag, . .	200
Anonymous.	

INTRODUCTION.

When we read a book it is desirable to have some knowledge of its author, and as my life-long friend, the Rev. George W. Gue, is about to present to the public a beautiful and patriotic work, entitled "OUR COUNTRY'S FLAG," it affords me great pleasure to have the privilege of introducing him to those who may read it and yet have never formed his acquaintance.

I presume no man living has known him as long and intimately as myself, and I am therefore qualified to speak. We were school-boys together, and for a number of years have been closely identified in the ministry.

He is a genial soul, has ever been earnest and enthusiastic, and the friends of his earlier life are not surprised that he is extensively and favorably known as a Methodist minister.

He was born February 27th, 1840, in Neville, Clermont County, Ohio, thirty miles above Cincinnati, on the banks of the Ohio river.

When ten years of age the family moved to Princeville, Peoria County, Illinois, where soon after his father, John W. Gue, died, leaving a wife, a daughter, and two sons, George being the oldest.

The mother, Mrs. J. T. Gue, a very intelligent, religious, and capable woman, carried on the mercantile business left by her husband for a number of years, making a comfortable support for the family and educating her children.

After receiving an academical education, at the age of nineteen years he was admitted into the ministry of the Methodist Episcopal church, becoming a member of the Peoria (now the Central Illinois) Conference, and was the youngest member ever received into that body.

In the central part of the State of Illinois he has spent the most of his life, faithfully laboring in the ministry, filling some of the most prominent pulpits in his conference with ability and marked success, being recognized by his brethren as a church-builder and successful financier.

In 1862, when the war-spirit was dominant in the land, extending to every loyal home, until city, village, and hamlet were thrilled with holy patriotic excitement, he enlisted as a private soldier, but in a short time was promoted to the Chaplaincy of the 108th Regiment Illinois Volunteers, and for three years in that capacity did good and faithful service. He was twenty-two years of age when commissioned, being the youngest Chaplain ever mustered into the United States Army, and was highly respected among the officers and men with whom he served.

Hon. John Warner, late Mayor of the city of Peoria, Illinois, and the first Colonel of the 108th Regiment, wrote of him, saying:

"Chaplain Gue was with his regiment on every march and in every battle, always at his post, bearing away the wounded and helping to cover up the dead. He was loved by every man in the regiment, who would have fought and died for him at any time."

Mr. Gue remained the Chaplain of that regiment for three years, and at the close of the war returned with a small fragment of what was once a splendid organization. They returned to Peoria, August, 1865, the same city where three years before they were mustered into the United States service.

For years Mr. Gue has been an active Grand Army man, serving the most of the time as Post Chaplain, and during the year 1889 he was Chaplain of the Department of Illinois of the G. A. R., and for years has been familiarly known as Chaplain Gue.

He has ever been a staunch friend of the Union and passionately fond of the FLAG — never happier than when preaching beneath its folds. This is one of his familiar sayings: "To me nothing is above the Stars and Stripes save the Cross of Jesus Christ."

With a fervor characteristic of the man, he has taken a deep and active interest in placing our Country's Flag upon schoolhouses and churches as far as his influence could aid in this direction.

To him for years the flag has been a special theme, ever delighting to speak of it in his sermons and addresses to secular and Sunday-Schools; but in his orations on special occasions he appears to the best advantage upon this theme. With a soul all aglow with patriotic fire, holding up the flag, portraying its beauties, and proclaiming its meaning, he has exhibited a wonderful power over his audiences in awakening in their hearts a love for the old flag.

For several years it has been known to a few of his friends that he has been gathering materials, consisting of poems, etc., on the American flag, with the thought of at some time placing them in book form. This has met the approval of many interested in him, who have urged the publication of the work, and this he has finally done.

It was a task requiring a vast amount of time and work, and involving a large expenditure of money, but it is just such a volume as is needed at the present time, and the publication of it cannot fail to do good.

Hoping this effort will be crowned with success, I am always his friend,

REV. C. W. AYLING,

Preface.

The flag of the United States of America — the Stars and Stripes — is a banner dearly loved by many millions of freemen. It is truly the emblem of the free and the brave. For more than a century it has waved triumphantly on every high sea and been hailed by lovers of true liberty in every land.

It is beautiful in painting, hanging in the drawing-room; beautiful when engraven by the sculptor on the granite rock, but far more beautiful when waving aloft from flag-staff or mast-head as the emblem of American liberty. It is glorious in the memories that cluster about it; glorious in the inspirations it awakens; glorious in its power to call the nation to arms to defend it from its foes; glorious on land and sea, where our proud victories have been won. Dear old flag, emblem of freedom! Oppressions die where it waves, and wrong can never triumph beneath its folds.

A million of men, out of the purest principles of patriotism, have surrendered everything dear to them and laid down their lives to maintain the honor of "Our Flag" and preserve the institutions it represents. Shall we of this generation, who enjoy protection under its folds, fail to appreciate what it means and what it cost?

The United States of America has but one flag — "The Stars and Stripes" — and there is no room in our republic for any other. It is the only one that should ever be carried in processions on our streets or wave over the homes and public buildings of our nation. In every school-room and over every pulpit this flag should be unfurled as an emblem of our Christian civilization and a lesson of patriotic devotion to all the institutions of this great American republic. To this end this souvenir is sent out on its mission among the people, believing that no more suitable or profitable present could be given by parents to children or friend to friend. Its very presence in the home will be a lesson of loyalty.

The design of this book is not intended to extol the soldier, but the flag. Care has been taken to keep the thought of the flag constantly in view in every selection. It is high-toned in every respect; and while designed to cultivate loyalty to our country and patriotic devotion to her institutions, it is entirely free from political, sectional, and sectarian prejudice.

This book comprises all the best poems on the American flag, both old and new, with extracts from speeches, also many mottoes and sayings. The engravings are all original, and of the finest workmanship. While Solomon's words are in this day literally true, "of making many books there is no end," still there is room and need for just such a publication as this.

Yours truly,

GEORGE W. GUE.

Acknowledgment.

The poems and other selections used in this publication have been gathered from many sources, and the most of them were covered by copyright. It has taken a great deal of time and pains to find the authors and publishers, and obtain their permission to use the articles presented in this book.

In the index the names of the authors, as far as it was possible to obtain them, have been given. I now take this opportunity of recognizing the publishers who have kindly permitted me to select and use such pieces from their publications as have suited my fancy.

I am especially indebted to Comrade J. C. O. Redington, of Syracuse, New York, who kindly furnished me about twenty of the most valuable poems in this collection, and many of them are his own production. He also rendered other service that I now take pleasure in this public manner of recognizing. He is the publisher of the *Acme Haversack*, a monthly publication of songs and patriotic eloquence.

I also wish to mention the publishing-house of S. Brainard's Sons, Chicago, Illinois, who gave me permission to use the following poems, on which they hold the copyright: "The Soldier's Pride," "Stand Up for the Flag," "The Stars and Stripes of Old," "Wrap the Flag Around Me, Boys," and "Our Flag and the Union Forever." They are the publishers of an excellent book, entitled "Our War Songs, North and South," also jobbers and importers of American and foreign music.

The elegant poem, "Flag of Our Country," is from the Cyclopædia of British and American Poets, and is inserted by permission of the publishers, Harper Brothers, New York.

With the consent of the Excelsior Publishing Company, 29 and 31 Beekman street, New York, I have taken from Burdett's Recitations and Readings two prose selections, one, "The Stars and Stripes," the author of which is unknown, and the other, by Rev. Henry Ward Beecher, entitled the "American Flag."

"The Stripes and Stars," by Edna Dean Proctor, is from a beautiful book of poems, called "Bugle Echoes," by D. F. Browne, who most cheerfully granted the privilege of reprinting it here.

"The History of Our Country's Flag" was written especially for this book, by Rev. Addis Albro, D. D., of Utica, New York, who deserves great credit for the time and pains he has taken in gathering the facts, and carefully writing this concise history of the United States Flag.

"Our Country's Flag" was composed for this work by Rev. D. A. Perrin, M. A., of Flanigan, Illinois, who is the author of several fine poems, and has published a souvenir entitled "Faith at the Cross."

"Our Honored Flag" and "Our Country's Flag on God's Sacred Altar" were written for this book, by request, by Mr. James W. Temple, of Victoria, Illinois.

"Our National Banner," written by William Dexter Smith, Jr., is from the "Patriotic Reader," a splendid work on patriotism, compiled by General Henry B. Carrington — a book that should be in all our schools. The poem is printed in this collection by permission of the author.

Professor J. Howard Wert, a poet of recognized ability, is the author of "Our Hallowed Flag," which is used in this work by his permission.

"Hurrah for the Flag," a part of which is here inserted, was composed by Miss M. H. Howliston, and is used by permission of the publishers, A. S. Barnes & Co.

When this book was ready for the press, and only waiting for a couple of the last engravings, I noticed, in reading the supplement to the "Encyclopædia Britannica," a reference to a publication entitled "The Flag of the United States and other National Flags," by George Henry Preble, of the United States Navy. I ordered the work, and found a number of extracts from speeches and sayings of representative men regarding the flag; these I have used in part, including a few verses suitable for this publication. With each quotation proper credit has been given.

I am also glad that I can publish in this book a couple of excellent poems by Rev. John Hogarth Lozier, of Mt. Vernon, Iowa, who was Chaplain of the 37th Regiment Indiana Infantry and Chaplain-in-Chief of the First National Encampment G. A. R., 1866. The poems he has given are, "Our Flag is Still Advancing" and "My Father's Flag and Mine," the song of the sons and daughters of veterans.

By a number of other persons, whose names I cannot give, I have been assisted in many ways in compiling this book, and I feel exceedingly grateful to all for the aid and encouragement thus given.

GEORGE W. GUE.

ROCK ISLAND, ILLINOIS.

THE HISTORY OF OUR COUNTRY'S FLAG.

REV. ADDIS ALBRO, LL. B., D. D.

In the whole universe of matter and mind, revelation is fundamental to existence. All nature is eloquent in the outward manifestation of internal character. It is instinctive of nature to unfold in varied order and beauty the marvelous harmonies with which it is endowed. In fact, nature itself is a sublime manifestation of the creative mind, and is everywhere symbolic of omnific power, wisdom, and goodness.

Man, who is exponential of his Creator, is vocal with this spirit of revelation. His character, invisible like that of his Maker, must be revealed. All of his actions tend in this direction. His most important means of communication is by words, which are signs of ideas inwardly conceived.

In the state where man is viewed as a member of society this same spirit obtains. The national life must be revealed. Underlying the nation are principles involved in its foundation, development, and preservation. These are sacred to the nation, and are expressed in its songs, embodied in its history, memorialized in its monuments, and inscribed upon its banners.

As expressive of principles vital to its existence, every order, society, or institution has its symbol. No age or nation has existed without its appropriate insignia. By an emblem the adherents of a party, faith, or union may express principles which might require volumes to make clear. Such an emblem is the cross, which symbolizes the entire Christian system. From time immemorial the FLAG, in some of its varied and numerous forms, has been prominent as an insignia. At the present time it is the ensign of most, if not all, of the nations of the earth.

The history of the American Flag is intensely interesting, and should be carefully studied. Early in their history the colonists used the royal ensign of England, which they variously modified as to form, color, and figure. At one time a special flag was established for New England, and consisted of a white field with a cross of St. George. In the center of this flag was inscribed "J. R."—*Jacobus Rex*—surmounted by a crown. In the beginning of the revolution a variety of flags was displayed, many of which bore some patriotic motto, such as "Liberty," "Liberty and Union," etc. In some instances these mottoes were defiant of the English government. After the battle of Lexington the troops of Connecticut displayed a flag on which was the arms of the colony, with the legend, "*Qui transtulit sustinet.*" After the battle of Bunker Hill a flag was unfurled containing on the obverse side the motto of Connecticut, and, on the reverse side the words, "*An Appeal to Heaven.*" Among the various flags borne by military companies during the revolution, the rattlesnake flag was, perhaps, among the most notable. It was displayed in at least two designs. In one form the snake had thirteen rattles, and under it was the injunction, "*Don't Tread on Me.*" In the other, the snake was in thirteen pieces, and below it was the legend, "*Join or Die.*"

In 1775 a committee appointed by Congress assembled at Cambridge to consider the subject of a flag for the colonies. They recommended the retention of the Union Jack, "representing the yet recognized sovereignty of England," and united with it thirteen stripes, alternate red and white, "emblematic of the union of the thirteen colonies against its tyranny and oppression." On January 2d, 1776, Washington hoisted this flag over the camp at Cambridge, and it was saluted with thirteen guns and thirteen cheers. The first flag, however, that bore thirteen stripes, as symbolic of the thirteen colonies, was invented by Abram Markoe, of Philadelphia, in the summer of 1775, and may have influenced the committee in the arrangement of the flag of 1775.

In June, 1777, a committee appointed by Congress to confer with General Washington concerning a design for a national flag reported the result of its work to Congress, which passed, without debate, on June 14th, the following: "Resolved, That the flag of the thirteen United States be thirteen stripes, alternate red and white; that the union be thirteen stars (white) in a blue field, representing a new constellation." This is the first and only record of the establishment of a national flag for the United States of America. The idea of the flag is thus given: "The red tells of the blood shed by our forefathers for their country; the blue, of the heavens and their protection; and the stars represent a new constellation of states." The blue of the field represents steadfastness, faith, and love; the red denotes courage, daring, and defiance; and the white is symbolic of integrity and purity. The flag, on the whole, was a blending of the desirable features of the various flags previously displayed by the colonists. The first flag of this pattern was made by Mrs. John Ross, 239 Arch street, Philadelphia. The residence occupied by Mrs. Ross, in which the first flag was made, still stands (1890) in Philadelphia, an object of interest to all.

After the recognition of the independence of the United States of America by Great Britain, the stars and stripes became recognized throughout the world as the symbol of a new nation. It was first displayed in England by the American painter, Copley, on December 5th, 1782. It was first hoisted in a British port at Downs, on February 3d, 1783, by the ship Bedford. Robert Gray, in 1788-90, first carried the American flag around the world.

It is related that "the first military incident connected with the stars and stripes belongs to Fort Stanwix, afterwards known as Fort Schuyler, and now the site of the city of Rome, New York, and occurred August 3d, 1778. When the enemy appeared before it the garrison was without a flag, but their patriotism and ingenuity soon supplied one. Sheets were cut up to form the white stripes, bits of scarlet cloth were joined for the red, and the blue ground for the stars was composed of a camlet cloak, furnished by Captain Abraham Swarthout. Before sunset this curious mosaic standard was floating over one of the bastions."

On January 13th, 1794, by act of Congress, after the admission of Vermont and Kentucky into the Union, the number of stars and stripes was increased to fifteen. This was the flag that inspired Francis Scott Keys, when a captive, to write the "Star-Spangled Banner."

On the admission of Indiana, in 1816, a committee was "appointed to inquire into the expediency of altering the flag of the United States." While the committee was deliberating, Captain Samuel Chester Reid, of the Navy, a son of Lieutenant John Reid, of the English Navy, was requested to make a design for our flag "without destroying its distinctive character." He recommended the reduction of "the number of stripes to thirteen, and that the stars be increased to the number of States, and be formed into one great star, whose brilliancy should represent their union; also that a star should be added to this constellation for every new State admitted." After considerable debate and delay, Congress, on April 4th, 1818, enacted: "That from and after the Fourth of July next the flag of the United States be thirteen horizontal stripes, alternate red and white; that the union have twenty stars (white) in a blue field; that on admission of every new State to the

Union one star be added to the union of the flag, and that such addition should take effect on the Fourth of July next succeeding such admission." This act was approved by the President on the day of its passage. The first flag conforming to this provision was made by Mrs. Reid, "the wife of its gallant designer, and had the stars arranged as one great star." This flag was hoisted over the House of Representatives, in Washington, D. C., April 14th, 1818, notwithstanding the law was not to go into effect until the Fourth of July following.

It will be noticed that Congress did not fix the kind or order of the stars placed upon the flag. The original design of the flag of 1777, as drawn in pencil by General Washington, and presented as a pattern to Mrs. Ross, required six-pointed stars. At the suggestion of Mrs. Ross that five-pointed stars would be more symmetrical, the design was changed. Since then custom makes the star five-pointed. The constellation in the original flag was irregular, which is believed to be the intent of the law of 1777, which established the flag. Since that time the form of the constellation has varied with the tastes of the people. By the War Department the stars in the union are usually arranged so as to form one large star of great brilliancy—symbolic of the grandeur of our Union of States. In the Navy the stars are arranged in straight lines, perpendicular and horizontal. Sometimes on other flags the stars are placed in a circle—significant of endless union. By a recent order of the Secretary of War, on and after July 4th, 1890, the stars are to be arranged in horizontal and perpendicular lines. Each horizontal line will contain seven stars. The bureau of equipment of the Navy Department has arranged, and the government accepted, that the field of the flag shall contain six horizontal rows of seven stars each, with an extra star at the upper left-hand corner of the field. After July 4th, 1891,

Wyoming's star will be placed at the lower left-hand corner. Until July 4th, 1891, the order is:

*   *   *   *

*

*

*   *   *   *   *

*   *   *

In designing a flag the width should be two-thirds of the length. The field, which is blue, should be one-third the length of the flag, and cover the width of seven stripes. Of the thirteen stripes seven are red. The stars, equal in number to the States of the Union, are white, and, by custom, five-pointed.

Our flag is the distinctive symbol of our nationality, and proudly and majestically waves, the ensign of a people whose civilization is second to none on the face of the earth.

From "O r Youth."]

BIRTHPLACE OF THE AMERICAN FLAG.

On one of the principal streets of Philadelphia stands a little two-and-one-half story building in a neighborhood with no companion of its kind, where ground is valuable. All around it big warehouses rear their heads, but amid the bustle and hurry

Birthp n of the A   n

and clash and clamor of commerce the little house modestly stands, and thus far has received scant reverence as the birthplace of the Star-Spangled Banner which now so triumphantly waves

"O'er the land of the free
And the home of the brave."

Congress, by resolution of June 14th, 1777, authorized the creation of the first flag of the United States thus:

" Resolved, That the flag of the thirteen United States be thirteen stripes, alternate red and white; that the union be thirteen stars (white) in a blue field, representing a new constellation."

The idea of the flag has thus been given: "The red tells of the blood shed by our forefathers for their country; the blue, of the heavens and their protection, and the stars represent a new constellation of states." The idea was taken from the constellation Lyra, which signifies harmony. The blue of the field was taken from the edges of Covenanters' banner, significant of the league and covenant against oppression, involving the virtues of vigilance, perseverance, and justice. The thirteen stripes and stars showed the number of the united colonies.

The whole was a blending of the various flags previous to the Union flag — the red one of the army and the white one of the floating batteries. The red color denotes daring and defiance, and the white purity.

After the passage of the resolution a committee of Congress,

which then met in Philadelphia, accompanied by General Washington, called upon Mrs. John Ross, a well-known milliner, living at 239 Arch street. They were received in her back parlor, and she was engaged to make a flag from a drawing made by General Washington with a pencil, and in that same room the work was completed.

Since then the house has undergone many changes of owners, but that little room has been preserved in its original condition, and so have the other portions of the dwelling, except that the necessary changes have been made in the front apartments to transform them into a beer-saloon.

The dingy back parlor where General Washington's fingers traced the outlines of the first emblems of American independence is a small room. Two windows with heavy sashes divided into small squares furnish it with light. In one corner is an old-fashioned cupboard, and an old-time fire-place is still surrounded by blue and white tiles, which plainly show that Mrs. John Ross was a lady of no mean position, and that her little home made pretensions to style.

Mrs. A. Mund, present owner of the historic building, assures us that no change will be made while she is alive. Large sums have been offered for the lot and also for the tiles around the fire-place. Visitors are welcome, and gladly shown the little back parlor.

CHARLES J. BUDD.

[From the "Inter-Ocean."]

DESECRATION OF THE FLAG.

A bill was reported to the National House of Representatives which every citizen who reveres the starry banner of National freedom will endorse. It reads:

"Be it enacted by the Senate and House of Representatives of the United States, in Congress assembled, That any person or persons who shall use the National flag, either by printing, painting, or affixing on said flag, or otherwise attaching to the same, any advertisement for public display or private gain shall be guilty of a misdemeanor, and on conviction thereof in the District Court of the United States shall be fined in any sum not exceeding fifty dollars, or imprisonment not less than thirty days, or both, at the discretion of the court."

ANONYMOUS.

MAGNIFYING THE FLAG.

Fervent devotion to the Star-Spangled Banner becomes a matter of course with all loyal Americans when war is on. But in the piping times of peace love of country is apt to wax cold, and the flag to be regarded with no more emotion than the primrose inspired in the breast of the man of whom Wordsworth sang —

> " A primrose by the river brim,
> A yellow primrose was to him;
> And it was nothing more."

Hence whatever in these tranquil days tends to stimulate the patriotic sentiment, to quicken affection for the flag, is deserving of the heartiest encouragement. Of late, it is gratifying to note, there has been manifest a disposition on the part of our people to honor the flag as it has never been honored before in time of peace. A bill was passed at the last session of the New York Legislature authorizing the purchase by the local authorities of the American colors, to the end that they may be flung to the breeze above the public school buildings. Early in the spring one of the Grand Army Posts at the Capital presented a beautiful flag to the High School, and there have been many similar presentations of late in various parts of the State and the country.

Of related significance is the bill which was lately reported to Congress from the Judiciary Committee, having for its object to prevent the desecration of the National flag. It provides that "any person who shall use the National flag, either by printing, painting, or affixing on said flag, or otherwise attaching to the same, any advertisement for public display or private gain shall be guilty of a misdemeanor, and on conviction thereof in the District Court of the United States shall be fined in any sum not exceeding fifty dollars, or imprisonment not less than thirty days, or both, at the discretion of the court." Doubtless some people will object to this measure, characterizing it as sentimental. But the majority of Americans will heartily approve of it. A people that allows its flag to be used for a display of advertisements connives at its degradation, and does not deserve to have a country. General Dix's famous "shoot-him-on-the-spot" order, looking to the preservation of the honor of the flag, did as much as anything in his long and illustrious career to commend him to the regard of his countrymen. But why place so much stress on the matter of keeping the flag flying if it is not something worthy of veneration? And if it is something worthy of veneration, then an advertisement insults it. The person who would advertise his wares on the flag of our Union would, if an opportunity offered, most likely tack one of his hand-bills on God's altar. There's a place for everything. The best place for an advertisement is in a newspaper.

It is the plain duty of all public-spirited Americans to do their best to make the rising generation feel an enthusiasm for the flag; to inspire in the hearts of the boys and girls of to-day so deep an affection and admiration for it in all that it implies that they shall grow up thorough-going patriots, who, if need be, will defend it with their lives. Let the revival of interest in the flag increase. It is a good sign. It indicates that this age of great material prosperity here in America is still an age when the virtue of patriotism is in a vigorous condition.

ANONYMOUS.

OUR COUNTRY'S FLAG.

Our country's flag revere,
Ye people far and near,
    On land and sea;
Stars that shall never fade,
With glorious stripes array'd,
By our forefathers made,
    For all our free.

Our country's fair ensign,
Thrice noble its design,
    It's triumphs sing;
Pride of our native land,
Joy of a mighty band,
Beneath we take our stand —
    Our tribute bring.

Preserv'd in peace and war,
Throughout our land afar,
    Our starry flag;
By comrades borne for us,
Thro' wars vic-to-ri-ous,
To us made glo-ri-ous,
    Our country's flag.

Hail, image of the skies,
O'er our proud land to rise,
    Resplendent, fair;
Renowned in his-to-ry,
Of brightest des-ti-ny,
Let songs of fe-al-ty
    Swell on the air.

God bless the rank and file,
With His benignant smile,
   Pledged to the flag;
Long may our banner wave,
O'er land our fathers gave,
Let all unite to save
   Our heritage.
          Rev. A. D. Perrin, M. A.

DANIEL WEBSTER ON "OUR FLAG."

"When the standard of the Union is raised and waves over my head — the standard which Washington planted on the ramparts of the Constitution — God forbid that I should inquire whom the people have commissioned to unfurl it and bear it up! I only ask in what manner, as an humble individual, I can best discharge my duty in defending it."

[For "Patriot Reader."]

OUR NATIONAL BANNER.

O'er the high and o'er the lowly
Floats that banner, bright and holy,
    In the rays of freedom's sun;
In the nation's heart embedded,
O'er our Union, newly wedded,
    One in all, and all in one.

Let that banner wave forever,
May its lustrous stars fade never,
    Till the stars shall pale on high.
While there's right the wrong defeating,
While there's hope in true hearts beating,
    Truth and freedom shall not die.

As it floated long before us,
Be it ever floating o'er us,
    O'er our land from shore to shore.
There are freemen yet to wave it,
Millions who would die to save it,
    Wave it, save it, evermore.

                WILLIAM DEXTER SMITH.

THE NUMBER AND ORDER OF STARS IN OUR COUNTRY'S FLAG.

By the order of Secretary Proctor, the union of the National flag in use in the Army and Navy consists, after July 4th, 1890, of forty-two white stars in six rows of seven stars each, in a blue field.

OUR FLAG.

The patriot, Wendover of old,
Suggested for our starry fold —
    The standard of the free —
Alternate stripes of white and red
In a blue field, like that o'er head,
    To float o'er land and sea.

He saw the soft stars shining through
The radiant realm of azure hue —
    A hint by nature given
To statesmen true, and brave, and wise —
And copied from the glowing skies
    The flag he saw in heaven.

Our fathers looked to heaven on high,
And transcribed from the starlit sky
    The beautiful design;
The blue, sprinkled with points of light,
To lead us in the path aright,
    Where lamps immortal shine.

The flag that waves from spire and mast,
Though baptized in the battle blast,
    May fly without surcease,
A light upon the land and sea,
A promise and a prophecy
    Of centuries of peace.

                            ANONYMOUS.

FREEDOM'S FLAG.

Our flag means, then, all that our fathers meant in the Revolutionary war. It means all that the Declaration of Independence meant; it means all that the Constitution of our people — organization for justice, for liberty, and for happiness — meant. Our flag carries American ideas, American history, and American feelings. Every color means liberty; every thread means liberty; every form of star and beam or stripe of light means liberty — not lawlessness, not license, but organized constitutional liberty. Liberty through law, and laws for liberty. Accept it, then, in all its fullness of meaning. It is not a painted rag. It is a whole National history. It is the Constitution. It is the government. It is the free people that stand on the government, on the Constitution. Forget not what it means; and for the sake of its ideas be true to your country's flag.

HENRY WARD BEECHER.

THE AMERICAN FLAG.

When Freedom, from her mountain height,
    Unfurled her standard to the air,
She tore the azure robe of night,
    And set the stars of glory there.
She mingled with its gorgeous dyes
The milky baldric of the skies,
And striped its pure, celestial white
With streakings of the morning light;
Then, from his mansion in the sun,
She called her eagle-bearer down,
And gave into his mighty hand
The symbol of her chosen land.

Majestic monarch of the clouds!
    Who rear'st aloft thy eagle form
To hear the tempest trampings loud,
    And see the lightning lances driven,
When strive the warriors of the storm,
    And rolls the thunder-drum of heaven!
Child of the Sun, to thee 'tis given
    To guard the banner of the free!
To hover in the sulphur smoke,
To ward away the battle stroke,
And bid its blendings shine afar,
Like rainbows on the cloud of war,
    The harbinger of victory.

Flag of the brave! thy folds shall fly,
The sign of hope and triumph high;
When speaks the signal trumpet tone,
And the long line comes gleaming on,
E're yet the life-blood, warm and wet,

Has dimmed the glistening bayonet,
Each soldier's eye shall proudly turn
To where thy sky-born glories burn;
And, as his springing steps advance,
Catch war and vengeance from the glance;
And when the cannon-mouthings loud
Heave in wild wreaths the battle-shroud,
And gory sabres rise and fall,
Like shoots of flame on midnight's pall —
 Then shall thy meteor-glances glow,
And cowering foes shall shrink beneath
 Each gallant arm that strikes below
That lovely messenger of death.

Flag of the seas! on ocean's wave
Thy stars shall glitter o'er the brave;
When death, careering on the gale,
Sweeps darkly round the bellied sail,
And frighted waves rush wildly back,
Before the broadside's reeling track,
Each dying wanderer of the sea
Shall look at once to heaven and thee,
And smile to see thy splendors fly
In triumph o'er his closing eye.

Flag of the free heart's hope and home!
 By angel hands to valor given;
Thy stars have lit the welkin dome,
 And all thy hues were born in heaven.
Forever float that standard sheet!
 Where breathes the foe but falls before us,
With Freedom's soil beneath our feet,
 And Freedom's banner streaming o'er us.

JOSEPH RODMAN DRAKE.

[From "Hildreth's History of the United States"]

OUR COUNTRY'S FLAG — WHEN ADOPTED BY CONGRESS.

The United States Flag, with its original thirteen stars and stripes, was adopted by Congress June 14th, 1777.

FIFTEEN STRIPES AND FIFTEEN STARS.

The bill to change the United States flag from its original design of thirteen stripes and thirteen stars was approved by the Congress of the United States January 13th, 1794, and reads as follows: "Be it enacted, etc., That from and after the first day of May, one thousand seven hundred and ninety-five, the flag of the United States be fifteen stripes, alternate red and white; that the union be fifteen stars (white) in a blue field."

For twenty-three years the flag of the United States carried fifteen stripes and fifteen stars. But Congress, on April 14th, 1818, passed an act to establish the flag of the United States:

"SECTION 1. Be it enacted, etc., That from and after the fourth day of July next the flag of the United States be thirteen horizontal stripes, alternate red and white; that the union have twenty stars (white) in a blue field.

"SEC. 2. And be it further enacted, That on the admission of every new State into the Union one star be added to the union of the flag; and that such addition shall take effect on the fourth day of July next succeeding such admission."

THE SOLDIER'S PRIDE.

All hail to thee, thou grand old flag,
    Still floating o'er the free,
Now soiled and torn by ruthless hands,
    Thou'rt doubly dear to me.

When in my boyhood's early years
    I saw thee first unfurled,
I deemed thee then the pride of earth,
    The glory of the world.

And when in later years I stood
    In busy haunts of men,
And saw thee float o'er field and flood,
    Old flag, I loved thee then!

But now, when in thy glorious light
    No slave can cringe or bow,
My father's and my country's flag,
    I love thee better now.

I'll bear thee up, thou dear old flag,
    Of origin divine,
Until upon thy azure fold
    A hundred stars shall shine.

Float on, old flag, until thy stripes
    Shall all the nations heal,
And tyrants over all the earth
    Shall thy just vengeance feel.

                  R. TOMPKINS

WHAT THE FLAG MEANS TO COMRADES.

Comrades, this flag has a meaning to us that it does not have to others; to them it is only an ensign of their country; to us it means all that is precious in our country's liberty — our homes, our lives, and all the blessings that will occur to the generations to come.

JOHN F. CHASE.

SWING OUT THE FLAG!

Swing out the flag, the brave old flag,
    Our grandest, best, and dearest
Symbol of light, freedom, and right,
    Whose stars shine out the clearest.
Swing out the flag, our brave old flag,
    The flag of song and story,
Through darkest night a beacon light,
    That led us on to glory.

Through battle's smoke the dawn awoke,
    The tyrant's chain was broken,
The country free, and liberty
    Rang through the land outspoken.
The world amazed upon it gazed,
    When on the breeze it floated.
Unfurled from light to dawning bright,
    By freedom's sons devoted.

When ruin wrought and rebels sought
    To blight its fame and story,
And quench the fires of patriot sires,
    Of freedom and of glory —
Then swept a thrill from hill to hill
    Of wrath and indignation,
From vale to crag, to save the flag
    From shame and degradation.

Men rushed to arms from town and farms,
    And even rebels trembled,
When freedom's hosts, our pride and boast,
    Beneath its stars assembled.
What could withstand that noble band,
    As brave as heaven is glorious,
Baptized in blood, they stemmed the flood,
    And bore it on victorious.

Then cheer the flag, the dear old flag,
    With fame its folds are laden,
With loud hurrahs and wild huzzahs,
    Each youth and gentle maiden!
Yes, cheer the flag, our dear old flag,
    That flag that failed us never;
From sea to sea, for liberty,
    May it wave on forever!

                        J. W. KINYON.

[From "Excelsior Reader, by perm"]

HENRY WARD BEECHER ON THE AMERICAN FLAG.

A thoughtful mind, when it sees a nation's flag, sees not the flag only, but the nation itself; and whatever may be its symbols — its insignia — he reads chiefly in the flag the government, the principles, the truth, the history which belongs to the nation that sets it forth.

When the French tri-color rolls out on the wind, we see France. When the new-found Italian flag is unfurled, we see resurrected Italy. When the other three-cornered Hungarian flag shall be lifted to the wind, we shall see in it the long-buried but never dead principles of Hungarian liberty. When the united crosses of St. Andrew and St. George on a fiery ground set forth the banner of Old England, we see not the cloth merely, there rises up before the mind the noble aspect of that monarchy, which, more than any other on the globe, has advanced its banner for liberty, law, and national prosperity.

Our nation has a banner, too; and wherever it streamed abroad men saw day-break bursting on their eyes, for the American flag has been the symbol of liberty, and men rejoiced in it. Not another flag on the globe had such an errand or went forth upon the sea carrying everywhere, the world around, such hope for the captive and such glorious tidings. The stars upon it were to the pining nations like the morning stars of God, and the stripes upon it were beams of morning light. As at early dawn the stars stand first, and then it grows light, and then, as the sun advances, that light breaks into banks of streaming lines of color, the glowing red and intense white striving together and ribbing the horizon with bars effulgent, so, on the American flag, stars and beams of many-colored light shine out together. And wherever the flag comes, and men behold it, they see in its sacred emblazonry no rampant lion and fierce eagle, but only light, and every fold significant of liberty.

The history of this banner is all on one side. Under it rode Washington and his armies; before it Burgoyne laid down his arms. It waved on the high lands at West Point; it floated over old Fort Montgomery. When Arnold would have surrendered these valuable fortresses and precious legacies his night was turned into day, and his treachery was driven away by the beams of light from this starry banner.

It cheered our army driven from New York in their solitary pilgrimage through New Jersey. It streamed in light over Valley Forge and Morristown. It crossed the waters rolling with ice at Trenton; and when its stars gleamed in the cold morning with victory, a new day of hope dawned on the despondency of the nation. And when at length the long years of war were drawing to a close, underneath the folds of this immortal banner sat Washington while Yorktown surrendered its hosts, and our revolutionary struggles ended with victory.

Let us, then, twine each thread of the glorious tissue of our country's flag about our heart-strings; and looking upon our homes, and catching the spirit that breathes upon us from the battle-field of our fathers, let us resolve, come weal or woe, we will, in life and in death, now and forever, stand by the Stars and Stripes.

They have been unfurled from the snows of Canada to the plains of New Orleans; in the halls of the Montezumas and amid the solitude of every sea; and everywhere, as the luminous symbol of restless and beneficent power, they have lead the brave to victory and to glory. They have floated over our cradles; let it be our prayer and our struggle that they shall float over our graves.

[By permission, from "Acme Haversack."]

GOD BLESS OUR FLAG.

God bless our glorious flag!
From vale to mountain crag
It floats in peace.
Proud banner of the free,
Ever triumphantly,
May earth expectant see
    Thy power increase.

              J. C. O. REDINGTON.

STAND UP FOR THE FLAG.

Stand up for the flag of your country,
    Our banner in peace and in war,
Determined, tho' rebels assail it,
    To cherish each stripe and each star;
As proudly to-day in its beauty
    It gives its bright folds to the sun
As when our forefathers baptized it,
    An emblem of victory won.

Stand up for the flag, let it never
    Be said of the brave and the free,
That riches and station and favor
    Its paltry usurper could be.
The red, white, and blue, how we love it,
    And guard it we will to the last —
Tho' rebels may stain and deface it,
    'Tis ours, for 'tis nailed to the mast.

Stand up for the flag of our country,
    Let liberty still be your cry,
Resolve in the strength of your fathers
    To place that banner on high;
The nations to come will behold it,
    Still floating o'er land and o'er sea,
This pledge of a people united,
    The beautiful flag of the free.

                      Mrs. M. S. Kidder.

[From the "Education" and Epworth L...]

THE FLAG OF THE UNITED STATES.

The American flag seems to hold above the nations the imperial ægis of a people's power. The flag is one of the forms of insignia by which our country shows forth and maintains its individuality; and its predominating use should and will powerfully appeal to the patriotism of all those who see in it the symbol, not only of their country's power, but its claims upon themselves. This influence reached its acme in the late war, when, like a rainbow in the cloud of battle, that flag, with its sign of hope and triumph, cheered the warriors amid the storm of leaden rain, and inspired them to the achievement of most brilliant victories. To defend that flag was to them something more than a duty; it was a joy, a coveted privilege akin to that which nerves the arm and directs the blow in defense of wife or child. Wherever that insignia floats, on the sea or on the land, it is to them the very Shekinah of their political love and faith. Among those who lived in the stirring times of the civil war the reading of Sheridan's ride excites the highest enthusiasm, and the singing of the Star-Spangled Banner always arouses the purest patriotism. But now another generation has come on the stage. They can have no conception of what the flag has been to their parents; by them it is most often seen in processions of political parties, whose orators denounce their brothers as traitors. Upon the children of to-day must rest the burdens of to-morrow, and it is the duty of the people to insist that the full significance of the flag shall be familiar to them. Then, with the flag as an incentive, let the rising generation be fired with a zealous love for the land of their birth. The setting forth of this principle has been sadly neglected; but there is a remedy, and that remedy is to be found in the schools of America. The ability to correct and eradicate this growing evil rests with the teachers; to them is given an opportunity to apply this remedy. To-day we see our beautiful emblem placed in many of the schools and colleges of our land. If instructors do their duty there is no reason why we should not have in the rising generation an embodiment of the highest type of patriotism.

Is it not necessary, also, that the people in general show more interest and solicitude in this matter? Place the flag in the churches of our country, for is not the love of country next to that of God? There, in association with the church, let it remain constantly before the eye; then our voters will be influenced, through the preaching of the truth in connection with this symbol of purity and valor, to see in a truer and more reverential light the vastness of the responsibility devolving upon them in their duty to the government. When casting their votes the apparition of the church and flag will appear, and they will say: "I am an American, and to be true I must take my stand for the glory of God, the protection of home, and the highest good of my native land."

The manner of celebrating our holidays must also be brought back to the original idea, from which it has so degenerated.

Then, with the flag waving high over all, let the people feel that this great country is their country; that they have a personal proprietorship in the lustre of her history, the honor of her name, the inviolability of her constitution and laws, and the magnitude and beneficence of her civil, social, and religious institutions.

LIZZIE T. GASSETT.

[For "Our Youth"]

THE FLAG'S BIRTHDAY.

The sails were out that morning, for Independence Day,
The air was mad with music, and every mast-head gay
With straining flags and pennants that fluttered to be free,
And cast a bright reflection upon the sunny sea.

Up spoke the lad beside me, with brave, brown eyes aflame:
"O, mother! can you tell me the gallant hero's name
Who flung the starry banner from ship or fortress wall
Full in the face of tyrants, the very first of all?"

My boy, do you remember how many a cloudless night
You've watched the vaulted heaven flash, star by star, a-light;
The Pole-star's steady beacon, the Pleiad's mild accord,
Or fierce Orion gleaming with firey belt and sword?

So the old patriot fathers up to the same far skies
Raised in the sleepless midnight their weary, anxious eyes —
Fain with the God of nations in silent prayer to speak,
Who fights with proud oppressors the battles of the weak.

And when in grave assemblage, beneath that storied tower
Whose throbbing bell had sounded the nation's natal hour,
The careworn Congress gathered, in faith that reached sublime,
To hear the march of freedom adown the field of time.

"Choose we," they said, "a standard, that, till the sun grow pale,
And summer time, and winter, and seed, and harvest fail,
Still in the hands of freemen a sacred trust shall be
To lead our country's armies to death or victory!"

Red, for the price of freedom, bled from the patriot's heart,
White, for his soul and honor, which life nor death could part;
Across the virgin banner the thirteen stripes they drew,
And left above, unsullied, a field of heavenly blue.

"Now, as the stars above us together show His praise,
Who set them in their courses and marked their trackless ways,
Let thus upon our banner our states united shine,
And a new constellation proclaim the hand divine!"

This said they in the council — these men of faith and deed —
And bade the scribe record it, that friend and foe might read;
The waiting west wind answered, and waves that beat in tune,
In seventeen seventy-seven, in the pleasant month of June.

Spoke Paul Jones, of the "Ranger" — a gallant captain he —
"To-day, my valiant comrades, our good bark puts to sea.
This be her boast forever, while keel shall cut the wave,
That first she wore these colors — the flag-ship of the brave!"

He sailed adown the harbor, while from his mast-head flew
The Stars and Stripes untarnished — the red, and white, and blue!
"God smite him," cried the captain, "with all the blasts that
 blow,
Who dares to strike that banner in face of any foe!"

On o'er the broad Atlantic he caught the trade-wind fair,
And braved the angry Lion within his island lair;
Up the blue Firth of Solway, on the bright river Dee,
Lord Selkirk's proud retainers before him bent the knee.

High soared the flag as backward he turned his prow again
To meet the host of Britain upon the open main —
Where 'mid the roar of battle, the billows' foam and surge,
Went down before that banner the standard of St. George!

Loud rang the shouts of welcome the people raised that day
They saw the gallant cruiser come beating up the bay ;
Her conquering colors tattered and rent by shot and gale
Sign of a storm-tossed Union whose cause should yet prevail !

The fathers of the nation sleep in their honored graves ;
The " Ranger's " dauntless captain no more may sail the waves ;
Yet o'er a land of freemen, unvexed by foreign foe,
Still floats the flag they lifted a hundred years ago !

O, Thou, whose hand almighty throughout the ages holds
The destiny of nations, guard Thou its sacred folds !
No traitor hand dissever the white and crimson bars !
No shadow of dishonor cloud o'er the silver stars !

The hands that bear that standard may never bribe allure !
The lips that swear it fealty with Thine own truth be pure !
So shall it wave, the symbol of love that knows not race,
But in each human brother discerns the Father's face !

MARY A. P. STANSBURY.

CROWN-PRINCE OF GERMANY AND THE UNITED STATES FLAG.

At the beginning of the Franco-Prussian War the Crown-Prince of Germany passed through Hamburg, on his way to the field. A young American girl, stopping with her parents at one of the hotels, hung a large American flag from the balcony, and, as the Prince passed by, waved her handkerchief. The Prince looked up, bowed, and ordered each regiment, as it passed by, to salute the Stars and Stripes.

I LOVE THEE, DEAR BANNER.

Oh, banner of glory! Oh, banner of light!
My soul is enraptured at the beautiful sight;
Thou art waving on high, the emblem of the free,
I love thee, dear banner, thou art waving for me.

I saw thee, thou beauty, 'mid the battle's thick smoke,
Thou didst inspire us when the nation awoke;
When the guns of rebellion sounded loud o'er the land,
Thy colors, they lead us, and nerved every man.

The foes of our nation sought thy glory to mar,
By dividing the union of the stripes and the stars;
But our gallant defenders triumphantly saved
The flag of our Union, the pride of the brave.

And now that the strife of battle has ceased,
We hail thee, and bless thee, thou banner of peace;
Thou shalt wave in thy splendor from steeple and dome,
The harbinger of peace, proclaiming Our Nation is One!

      REV. GEORGE W. GUE.

FLAG OF THE NOBLE.

Flag of the noble, free, and brave,
    With joy we see it streaming there;
No other flag deserves to wave
    So high in fields of light and air.
It's sanctified by sacrifice,
    With pride its glowing folds we see;
The prayers of millions daily rise,
    Forever float triumphantly!

                WILLIAM FREEMAN.

THE BEAUTIFUL FLAG OF THE FREE.

Flag of my country, the flag of the free,
Beautiful streamer, now dearer to me;
Peerless and stainless, triumphantly wave
Over a nation that knows not a slave.

Boast of the sires who bequeathed us a life,
Boast of the sons on the red field of strife;
Boast of the serf as he toils o'er the sea,
Hope of the world is the flag of the free.

Fled are the foes who thy beauty would mar,
Gone not one stripe, and effaced not one star;
Broken and humbled they turn unto thee,
Sighing for rest 'neath the flag of the free.

Victors and vanquished are one as of yore,
War's gory hand shall divide them no more;
Once they were brothers, and brothers they'll be,
Happy again 'neath the flag of the free.

Buried the past, they will toil to adorn
Freedom's domain for a nation unborn;
And when they fall, this their solace shall be,
Over them floats the dear flag of the free.

ANONYMOUS.

OUR FLAG ON THE ANDES MOUNTAINS.

On the Fourth of July, 1873, a party of American engineers, in pioneering the Oroya railroad from Lima across the Andes, raised "our flag" on a summit of the Andes seventeen thousand five hundred and seventy-four feet above the sea level, in snow knee-deep.

THE OLD FLAG.

Touch lightly the tatters of red, white, and blue,
All time-stained and soiled with the blood of the true ;
And the flag-staff as old as the colors are worn,
With the marks of the fingers in which it was borne !
Touch lightly the tatters, their splendor is bare,
All sun-steeped and faded their coloring rare ;
But tho' torn into ribbons, and gone every hue,
Our hearts will supply them, the red, white, and blue.

Touch lightly the tatters, for freedom bends o'er,
And she touches each hue into glory once more ;
And she gathers the shreds, and she waves them with might,
For union and valor, for God and the right !
Touch lightly the tatters ! she loves every shred,
And she holds them aloft over tyranny's head,
Where all brave with her smiling, wet with her tears,
They shall flutter in triumph undimmed thro' the years.

Touch lightly the tatters, they floated that day
Each blue-coated soldier went marching away ;
And in the gray dawn of the faint morning glow,
Pale Liberty's sentinels marched to and fro.
Oh proudly they floated, each sun-faded rag,
And brave was the soldier who stood by the flag ;
And dear were the eyes that grew dim as they gazed,
Where the emblem of loyalty proudly was raised.

Touch lightly the tatters, tho' listless they lie,
There once was a time when the stripes floated high;
When the noise of the battle fell thick on the ear,
And Freedom crouched lower, and trembled to hear —
When the boom of the cannon was sullen and long,
And the harsh voice of war fell discordant and strong,
And the bullet hissed home to the heart of the true,
And the soldier was dead — for the red, white, and blue!

Touch lightly the tatters, the sound of the drums,
As we look at their raggedness, fitfully come;
And the marching of footsteps away to the death,
And the flashing of swords, and the sharply drawn breath.
And after the valorous battle was done,
The death-tired faces upturned to the sun;
And we love every tatter, each wind-whistled rag,
For the sake of the comrades who died for the flag!

Touch lightly the tatters, the soldier boy lay
All faint on the battle-field, long miles away;
Unkissed by the lips that his dear name were crying;
Unknown to the love that would soften the dying;
And the death angel stalking so near to the place,
Came nearer, and bent o'er his strife-tired face,
Till he fell fast 'mid the strife, till they found him,
And laid him to rest with the flag wrapped around him.

Touch lightly the tatters, they never will fade!
Too dear was the price for their loveliness paid;
Too many the tears that lay thick where they lie,
Too many the faces upturned to the sky.
And as long as there's loyalty under the sun,
The flags will wave on for the deeds that were done;
The pride of our nation, forever it stands,
For Freedom will hold it in both willing hands.

Miss Minnie G. McArthur.

HOW TO CONSTRUCT OUR FLAG.

The United States flag has thirteen stripes and one star for every State in the Union. Each stripe should be half as many inches wide as the flag is feet long. The union (or field) should be one-third the length of the flag and covering seven stripes in width.

THE STARS AND STRIPES OF OLD.

We are a band of freemen, who love our native land,
To save it from rebellion we come with heart and hand;
We left our homes behind us, when Sumpter's tale was told,
To rally round our banner, the stars and stripes of old.

The rebel hosts may gather, with savage fury fight,
But they can never conquer our strength as in our right
We follow on triumphant where, on the breeze unrolled,
Waves high our glorious banner, the stars and stripes of old.

They mocked our peaceful labor, they scorn our patient toil,
But on their vain pretensions the blow shall soon recoil.
The men they have derided shall o'er their homes unfold
The banner they have scouted, the stars and stripes of old.

Our fathers fought for freedom, we will preserve their land,
Unbroken, undivided, it shall ever stand.
Until 'tis reunited we never again will fold,
The banner floating o'er us, the stars and stripes of old.

C. Jay.

RAISE THE STAR-GEMMED BANNER.

As we raise our country's banner, in the strength of youth are we
Bound to cherish what our fathers left us for our legacy.
Oh! raise the star-gemmed banner, 'tis the flag that makes us free,
The flag our patriot fathers, dying, gave to liberty.
  Raise, oh! raise the flag!
The flag our patriot fathers, dying, gave to liberty.

Stars and Stripes! ever proudly float, that millions yet to be
May arise to pay you homage, on the land and on the sea.
Prosperity and happy peace are blessing our dear land,
A beacon for oppressed of earth will fair Columbia stand.
  Raise, oh! raise the flag!
The flag our patriot fathers, dying, gave to liberty.

We now pledge our vows of fealty, to ever faithfully
Guard the precious birthright given in this land of liberty.
We'll hand it down unsullied in its fame from sire to son,
And sleep beneath its shadow when the goal of life is won.
  Raise, oh! raise the flag!
The flag our patriot fathers, dying, gave to liberty.

ADELAIDE GEORGE BENNETT.

THE FORT McHENRY FLAG EXHIBITED IN 1876.

The centennial anniversary of the adoption of the star-spangled banner, June 14th, 1877, was appropriately remembered in various parts of the United States. In Boston a patriotic demonstration was held in the Old South Meeting-house. The veritable flag of Fort McHenry, the original of Francis Scott Key's "Star-Spangled Banner," was displayed, and the song was sung by Mrs. Julia Houston West, the audience joining in the chorus.

HAIL OUR FLAG!

Now thy beauteous stripes are blazing, and thy stars with lustre glow,
And our hearts are filled with rapture none but freemen ever know.
How this crown of freedom's triumphs flings its radiance to the breeze.
'Mid the loud huzzas of millions from the oceans to the seas.

> Hail our flag! glorious flag! red, white, and blue!
> Noble souls have saved thee, bravest men and true;
> Who the grandest victories on earth have won,
> When they fought in freedom's dauntless ranks, from Grant to Washington.

How thy glorious folds have floated through fierce storms of shot and shell,
Till all torn in shreds and tatters o'er the spot where heroes fell!
Thou hast marched to mighty triumph with the bravest of the brave,
Who have nailed aloft thy freedom-stars forever more to wave.

HARRY C. BURNS.

FLAG OF OUR UNION FOREVER.

A song for "Our Banner," the watchword recall,
    Which gave the republic her station —
" United we stand, divided we fall!"
    It made and preserves us a nation.
The union of lakes, the union of hands,
    The Union of States none can sever!
The union of hearts, the union of hands,
    And the flag of our Union forever and ever,
    The flag of our Union forever!

What God in His infinite wisdom designed,
    And armed with national thunder,
Not all the earth's despots and factions combined
    Have the power to conquer or sunder.
The union of lakes, the union of hands,
    The Union of States none can sever!
The union of hearts, the union of hands,
    And the flag of our Union forever and ever,
    The flag of our Union forever!

Oh, keep that flag flying! the pride of the van!
    To all other nations display it!
The ladies for union are all to a — man!
    And not to the man who'd betray it.
Then the union of lakes, the union of hands,
    The Union of States none can sever!
The union of hearts, the union of hands,
    And the flag of the Union forever!

                              GEORGE P. MORRIS.

"There are two things holy — the flag which represents military honor, and the law which represents the national right."

VICTOR HUGO.

COLUMBIA'S FLAG.

Of all the flags that proudly float
    O'er Neptune's gallant tars,
Or wave on high in victory
    Above the sons of Mars,
Give us that flag, Columbia's flag,
    Pure emblem of the free,
Whose brilliant stars flashed through our wars,
    For truth and liberty.

Then dip it, lads, in ocean's brine,
    Greet it with three-times-three!
Columbia's flag shall henceforth shine,
    The banner of the sea.

Beneath its folds we fear no foes,
    Our hearts shall never quail,
With bosoms bare the storm we dare,
    And brave the battle's hail.
E'en when our decks with shot were ploughed,
    Their planks with gore dyed red,
Our gallant tars, firm at their posts,
    Ne'er paused to count their dead.

Then dip it, lads, in ocean's brine,
    Greet it with three-times-three!
The flag that was at Mobile made
    The banner of the sea.

Far o'er the sea to every clime
    This honored flag shall go,
And through all time its fame sublime
    With brighter hues shall glow.
For Freedom's own that flag is now,
    Its guardians freedom's sons,
And woe betide the insolent
    On whom they train their guns.

Then dip it, lads, in ocean's brine,
    Greet it with three-times-three!
The flag for which our tars have won
    Dominion on the sea.

Its enemies dispersed shall be
    Upon the land and main,
Its stars so bright mid storm and fight
    Will never shine in vain.
No foreign power nor treason rife
    Shall shake our courage keen,
We'll give our lives in deadly strife
    To hold that flag supreme.

Then dip it, lads, in ocean's brine,
    Greet it with three-times-three!
At last, thank God! our navy flies
    The banner of the sea.

[Written while in Mobile Bay by William Dinsmore, boatswain's mate on the " New Ironsides."]

[From "The Flag of the United States, a Poem"]

UNFURL THE GLORIOUS BANNER.

Unfurl the glorious banner,
    Which at Eutaw shone so bright,
And like a dazzling meteor swept
    Through the Cowpens deadly fight.
Sound, sound your lively bugles,
    Let them pour their loudest blast,
While we pledge both life and honor
    To stand by it to the last.

                      ANONYMOUS.

THE NATIONAL ENSIGN.

The national ensign, pure and simple, dearer to all our hearts at this moment, as we lift it to the gale and see no other sign of hope upon the storm-cloud which rolls and settles above it save that which is reflected from its own radiant hues — dearer, a thousand-fold dearer, to us all than ever it was before while gilded by the sunshine of prosperity and playing with the zephyrs of peace. It speaks for itself far more eloquent than I can speak for it. Behold it! Listen to it! Every star has a tongue. Every stripe is articulate. There is no language or speech where their voices are not heard. There's magic in the web of it. It has an answer for every question. It has a solution for every doubt and every perplexity. It has a word of good cheer for every hour of gloom or despondency. Behold it! Listen to it! It speaks of earlier and later struggles. It speaks of heroes and patriots among the living and among the dead.

But before all, and above all other associates and memories, whether of glorious men, or glorious deeds, or glorious places, its voice is ever of union and liberty, of the constitution and the laws. Behold it! Listen to it! Let it tell the story of its birth to these gallant volunteers as they march beneath its folds by day or repose beneath its sentinal stars by night. Let it recall to them the strange, eventful history of its rise and progress. Let it rehearse to them the wondrous tale of its trials and its triumphs in peace and war.

ROBERT C. WINTHROP.

October 3d, 1861.

THE STRIPES AND THE STARS.

O, Star-Spangled Banner! the flag of our pride,
Though trampled by traitors and basely defied,
Fling out to the glad winds your red, white, and blue,
For the heart of the North land is beating for you;
And her strong arm is nerving to strike with a will
Till the foe and his boastings are humbled and still.
Here's welcome to wounding, and combat, and scars,
And the glory of death for the stripes and the stars

From prairie, O, ploughman! speed boldly away,
There's seed to be sown in God's furrow to-day!
Row landward, lone fisher, stout woodman, come home,
Let smith leave his anvil, and weaver his loom,
And hamlet and city ring loud with the cry,
"For God and our country we'll fight 'till we die!"
Here's welcome to wounding and combat and scars,
And the glory of death for the stripes and the stars.

Invincible banner! the flag of the free,
Oh, where treads the foot that would falter for thee?
Or the hands to be folded, till triumph is won,
And the eagle looks proud, as of old, to the sun!
Give tears for the parting — a murmur of prayer
Then forward! the fame of our standard to share!
With welcome to wounding, and combat, and scars
And the glory of death for the stripes and the stars

O, God of our fathers! this banner must shine
Where battle is hottest, in warfare divine!
The cannon has thundered, the bugle has blown,
We fear not the summons, we fight not alone!
O, lead us, till wide from the gulf to the sea,
The land shall be sacred to freedom and thee!
With love for the oppressed, with blessing for scars,
One country; one banner — the stripes and the stars.
EDNA DEAN PROCTOR.

STAND BY THE OLD FLAG.

As a high private in Kirk's brigade, McCook's division, Army of the Ohio, I took part in the battle of Shiloh, Monday, April 7th, 1862. General Rousseau's brigade took the advance of our division early in the morning. We formed line in rear of Rousseau as supports, advancing as they did. Just before reaching an open field the enemy appeared to hold their ground with unusual determination. As we moved nearer the line engaged, the enemy gave way for a short distance, and we halted a few moments. Right at my feet lay a Captain, with "L. L."— Louisville Legion of Rousseau's brigade — on the lapel of his coat. His entire right forehead seemed to have been shot away. Comrade Baker, who stood beside me, bent down and poured some water into his mouth, when the fallen Captain slowly opened his eyes. As he did so he caught sight of the colors of our regiment, which happened to be almost over him. Without a tremor, in a low voice, he called out: "Stand by the old flag, boys, stand by the old flag," and immediately became unconscious. In a short time we were engaged with the enemy, and those words rang in my ears above the voice of battle. I had resolved to hunt up the brave Captain as soon as the battle was over, but was severely wounded myself and could not do so; but how often since have those words encouraged me, breathing as they did the unselfish thoughts of a patriot dying on the battle-field.

ROBERT M. WILSON.

THE STAR-SPANGLED BANNER.

Oh, say, can you see, by the dawn's early light,
    What so proudly we hailed at the twilight's last gleaming?
Whose broad stripes and bright stars, through the perilous fight,
    O'er the ramparts we watched, were so gallantly shining;
And the rocket's red glare, the bombs bursting in air,
Gave proof through the night that our flag was still there;
Oh, say, does that star-spangled banner yet wave
O'er the land of the free and the home of the brave?

On the shore, dimly seen through the mists of the deep,
    Where the foes haughty host in dread silence reposes,
What is that which the breeze, o'er the towering steep,
    As it fitfully blows, half conceals, half discloses?
Now it catches the gleam of the morning's first beam,
In full glory reflected, now shines on the stream;
'Tis the star-spangled banner; oh, long may it wave
O'er the land of the free and the home of the brave!

And where is the band who so vauntingly swore,
    'Mid the havoc of war and the battle's confusion,
A home and a country they'd leave us no more!
    Their blood has washed out their foul footsteps' pollution;
No refuge could save the hireling and slave
From the terror of flight, or the gloom of the grave;
And the star-spangled banner in triumph doth wave
O'er the land of the free and the home of the brave.

Oh, thus be it ever, when freemen shall stand
    Between their loved home and the war's desolation !
Blessed with victory and peace, may the heaven-rescued land
    Praise the power that hath made and preserved us a nation :
Then conquer we must, for our cause it is just,
And this be our motto, "In God is our trust."
And the star-spangled banner in triumph shall wave
O'er the land of the free and the home of the brave.
FRANCIS SCOTT KEY.

THE AUTHOR OF THE STAR SPANGLED BANNER

Francis Scott Key, the author of "The Star-Spangled Banner," was a lawyer by profession, and was born in Frederick county, Maryland, August 1st, 1779, and died in Baltimore, January 11th, 1843. The song which immortalized his name and became national was inspired by the author witnessing the bombardment of Fort McHenry, September 13th, 1814. The song was first published in the "Baltimore American," September 21st, 1814, a week after the battle, with these prefatory remarks:

"This song was composed under the following circumstances: Mr. F. S. Key left Baltimore in a flag of truce for the purpose of getting released from the British fleet a friend, and was temporarily detained, witnessing the bombardment of Fort McHenry. He watched the flag at the fort all day with anxiety; in the night he watched the bomb-shells, and at early dawn his eye was again greeted by the proudly waving flag of our country."

It was while pacing the deck of the cartel-ship "Minden," between midnight and dawn, that Key composed his song.

The Star-Spangled Banner was first sung in a small one-story frame house, occupied as a tavern, a house where players and soldiers congregated.

It was caught up in camps, and sung around the bivouac fires, whistled in the streets, and when peace was declared, and soldiers scattered to their homes, it was carried to thousands of firesides as the most precious relic of the war of 1812.

The flag of Fort McHenry, whose broad stripes and bright stars inspired Key's song, still exists in a tolerable state of preservation. The regulation size of the garrison flags at the present time is thirty-six feet fly and twenty feet hoist.

The flag of Fort McHenry, in its present curtailed dimensions, is thirty-two feet long and twenty-nine feet hoist. Undoubtedly, originally it was forty feet long — the shots of the enemy and time have combined to decrease its length.

Its great width is due to its having fifteen instead of thirteen stripes, each nearly two feet wide. It had fifteen five-pointed stars, each two feet from point to point, arranged in five indented parallel lines, three stars in each horizontal line. The union rests in the ninth stripe, which is red, instead of the eighth, a white stripe, as in our present flag. All the flags worn by the Navy and Army during the war of 1811-14 were made this way; in fact they were so arranged from 1794 to 1818.

This flag was exhibited in the naval department of the centennial exhibition, in Philadelphia, and again at the Old South Church, Boston, June 14th, 1877, the centennial anniversary of the passage by the Continental Congress of the act adopting the star-spangled banner as the emblem of the Confederated States.

There is no doubt as to the authenticity of this flag. It was preserved by Colonel Armsted, and bears his name and date of the bombardment. It has always remained in his family, and his widow, in 1861, bequeathed it to their youngest daughter, Mrs. Stuart Appleton, who, soon after the bombardment, was born in Fort McHenry under its folds. Mrs. Appleton died July 25th, 1878, and bequeathed the flag to her son, who now holds it.

A letter from Mrs. Caroline Purdy, of Baltimore, to Mrs. Appleton, describes the making of this historic flag:

"It was made by my mother, and I assisted her. The flag being so very large, my mother was obliged to obtain permission from the proprietor of a brewery to spread it out in their malt-house, and I remember seeing my mother down on the floor placing the stars. The flag, I think, contained four hundred yards, and we worked many nights until 12 o'clock to complete it in a given time."

RALLY ROUND THE OLD FLAG!

Rally round the "Old Flag!"
    "Banner of the free,"
Radiant with triumphs
    Won for liberty.
Emblem of hope and joy
    Unto all oppressed,
Equal rights everywhere,
    That all may be blessed.
In a grand and awful time
    We all are dwelling;
To be living is sublime,
    When on ages telling —
The power of liberty shall grow
Till all the earth shall know.

Don't forget the vast cost
    Freedom's flag to save,
Or the deeds that made it sure
    Evermore to wave.
Heroes fought in its defense,
    For it won renown;
Placed it where it proudly floats,
    Never to go down.
Flag of hope to earth's oppressed,
    Wave on in glory;
Cheering aching, suff'ring souls
    With freedom's story —
That bye and bye, to everyone,
A better day will come.

                COMRADE REDINGTON.

FOREVER FLOAT THE OLD FLAG!

Wherever Columbia's favored children turn,
In her peace and her prosperity all patriots may learn
What free institutions to ev'ry one will give,
Who is fortunate and favored under freedom's flag to live.

> Forever float the old flag, the red, white, and blue flag!
> The saved flag, the proud flag, the triumph-of-the-true flag!
> Our hearts ever cherish its valor-gilded field,
> And bless its defenders, too true to ever yield.

The old flag has cost earth's most mighty sacrifice;
From four years of deadly suffering the nation saw it rise,
Baptized in the blood of our noblest and our best;
But 'twas saved! and now it grandly shields the cause their
    deeds have blessed.

And what they've defended their children will preserve;
From our loyalty to flag and country we will never swerve.
The old flag, the bless'd flag of truth,
Is the flag to which we'll rally ev'ry day from early youth.

J. C. O. REDINGTON.

OUR FLAG OF THE FREE.

Bright banner of the free,
Still wave from sea to sea,
 Our Union's pride!
Flag that our father's bore
Amid the cannon's roar
By every sea and shore,
 For thee they died.

ANONYMOUS.

RALLY ROUND YOUR COUNTRY'S FLAG.

Every man must be for the United States or against it. There can be no neutrals in this war — only patriots or traitors. I express it as my conviction before God, that it is the duty of every American citizen to rally round the flag of his country.

STEPHEN A. DOUGLASS, 1861.

OUR FLAG.

O, banner that we love,
Fair as the heavens above,
   Flag of the free!
O'er our land ever wave,
Land of the true and brave,
Land where there breathes no slave
   From sea to sea!

Glowing with crimson dyes,
Like sunset's burning skies,
   O, banner fair!
Banded with snowy white,
Pure as the stars at night,
With thee, our heart's delight,
   What can compare?

Each star upon thy breast
Shall there forever rest,
   Glorious and free;
And all the winds that swell
Through every peaceful dell,
Where'er they go shall tell
   Our love for thee.

Flag of the brave and free,
Emblem of liberty,
   Banner we love!
Thanks for each radiant fold,
And every star of gold,
Freed from oppression's hold,
   Give God above.

              NINETTE M. LOWATER.

KEEP THE FLAG IN VIEW.

Ever keep before our eyes the "Glory Flag" of old!
The stars and stripes let every loyal heart with love enfold;
Preserved by such deep sacrifice as never can be told;
   Oh! keep the flag in view!

ANONYMOUS.

THE FIRST UNITED STATES FLAG AROUND THE WORLD.

The honor of being the first to carry "Our Country's Flag" around the world is assigned to the auspiciously and appropriately named ship, "Columbia," which, under command of Captain's Kendrick and Gray, circumnavigated the globe in 1789-90.

OUR FLAG IN THE SOUTH.

Across the chasm, dark and bloody,
    Where armed hate once cruel stood,
Let us build anew the union
    Of our common brotherhood.

Unfurl for us the Nation's banner,
    Flag of a land forever free;
We, too, would claim and share its glory,
    As it floats o'er land and sea.

In the days long past our fathers
    Stood beneath the flag's broad fold;
In the days to come our children
    Will, with yours, its fame uphold.

Thus, by friendship's ties united,
    We will change the bloody past
Into golden links of union,
    Blending all in love at last.

Thus beneath the one broad banner,
    Flag of the true, the brave, the free,
We will build anew the Union,
    Fortress of our liberty.

                        C. C. BAYLOR.

LIEUTENANT-GENERAL WINFIELD SCOTT AND THE UNITED STATES FLAG.

"I have served my country under the flag of the Union for more than fifty years; and as long as God permits me to live I will defend that flag with my sword, even if my own State assails it."

OUR FLAG OF LIBERTY.

Our flag, our flag, the grand old flag,
From mountain top, from towering crag,
O'er prairie wide, and inland seas,
In honor floats on every breeze;
And paints with tints that naught can tame
A monogram of living fame.
The flag our eyes are proud to see,
The grand old flag of liberty.

Our flag, our flag, without a stain,
That will be pure while right shall reign;
Long may its splendor brightly shine
On brow of liberty divine,
A harbinger the world to bless,
A glorious light from radiant West.
The flag our eyes are bound to see,
The grand old flag of liberty.

Our flag, our flag, in battle smoke,
Mid bayonet clash and sabre stroke,
Will onward lead a charging line —
An inspiration so sublime
That cowards c'an forget their fear —
And charge to death with loyal cheer.
That flag our eyes are proud to see,
The grand old flag of liberty.

Our flag, our flag, o'er land and sea,
Shall rule where heart of man is free,
It bids the despot cower in fear,
The slave to hope that freedom's near;
And loud proclaims the grand design
That equal rights on all shall shine.
The flag our eyes are proud to see,
Triumphant flag of liberty.

Our flag, our flag, the youth will stand
Around that flag, a loyal band,
With hearts as true as those of yore,
When patriot fathers bravely bore
That flag victorious toward the skies,
Its triumph won by sacrifice.
The flag our eyes are proud to see,
The grand old flag of liberty.
COLONEL S. D. RICHARDSON

THE FIRST UNITED STATES FLAG IN THE INTERIOR OF CHINA.

In 1877 our flag was unfurled for the first time one thousand miles in the interior of China.

THE UNITED STATES FLAG AT THE COMPLETION OF THE UNION PACIFIC RAILROAD.

When the tie connecting the Union Pacific railroad was laid, August 7th, 1868, the idea was suggested of erecting a monument commemorative of the event, and planting the national flag on the divide. On Sunday, August 9th, a company assembled at a point about seven hundred and twenty-five miles from Omaha. The Rev. Mr. Gierlow pronounced the following consecration service while the flag was being hoisted by a Mrs. Clayton:

"In the name of wisdom, strength, and beauty; in the name of faith, hope, and charity; in the name of the Holy Trinity, we consecrate this flag to the glory of God, the benefit of civilization, and the happiness of mankind; and may its ample folds protect us in the path of virtue, so that we may become worthy citizens of the land of the free."

The spot where this flag was planted is the true continental summit.

ONE FLAG ONLY.

Comrades! I am unmoved by any rancor or spirit of hatred. God forbid; but I am a Union soldier, and I love my flag, and I say here, and I will say everywhere, that for Americans there is but one flag — the flag of Bunker Hill, and Saratoga, and Yorktown; the flag of Lundy's Lane, Lake Champlain, and Erie, and New Orleans; the flag of Scott, McDonough, Perry, and Jackson; the flag of Lincoln, the flag of Hancock, the flag of Grant, the flag of Washington. It is the only flag which represents the right, and in our charity let us not forget the difference between right and wrong.

GENERAL DANIEL E. SICKLES.

[By permission, from Au...]

OUR GLORIOUS FLAG.

Out of the battle glare,
See, all the stars are there,
   Gleaming like gold.
Doubly its hues are blest,
Thousands have gone to rest,
Noblest, bravest, and best,
   Under its fold.

H. C. BALLARD.

THE FLAG OUR HERO BORE.

" Bring me the flag," the vet'ran said,
    " The flag I've held before,
The war-worn flag, the battle-flag,
    The flag our hero bore.
With tender care now take it down,
    And bring it to my side,
Tear not a shred of tattered folds —
    That flag's my joy and pride.

" On many a hard fought field, my boy,"
    Exclaimed the aged sire,
" I saw it wave victoriously
    'Mid shot, and shell, and fire ;
And when the bullet pierced my side —
    Though faint, my son, with pain —
I took that flag, that dear old flag,
    And spread it on the slain.

" When past, the sad and cruel war,
    My boy, I placed it there,
And as my voice will soon be hushed,
    I leave it in your care.
Oh, keep the flag," the vet'ran said,
    " My days on earth are o'er,
That starry flag, the war-scarred flag,
    The flag our hero bore "

                    I J. BIELBY.

From "The Flag of the United States," by P...

HAIL, TO OUR BANNER.

Hail to our banner, brave,
All o'er the land and wave,
   To-day unfurled!
No folds to us so fair,
Thrown on the summer air,
None can with thee compare,
   In all the world.

W. P. TILDEN.

OUR STAR-GEMMED BANNER — SPIRIT OF 1861.

God bless our star-gemmed banner, shake its folds out to the breeze,
From church, from fort, from house-top, o'er the city, on the seas ;
The die is cast, the storm at last has broken in its might ;
Unfurl the starry banner, and may God defend the right !

Too long our flag has sheltered rebel heart and stormy will ;
Too long has nursed the traitor who has worked to do it ill ;
That time is past, the thrilling blast of war is heard at length,
And the North pours forth her legions that have slumbered in their strength.

They have roused them to the danger, armed and ready forth they stand,
A hundred thousand volunteers, each with weapon in his hand ;
They rally round that banner, they obey their country's call,
The spirit of the North is up, and thrilling one and all.

'Tis the flag our sires and grandsires honored to their latest breath,
To us 'tis given to hold unstained, to guard in life or death ;
Time-honored, from its stately folds who has dared to strike a star
That glittered on its field of blue — who but traitors, as they are ?

Would to God it waved above us with a foreign foe to quell,
Not o'er brother faced to brother, urging steel, and shot, and shell;
But no more the choice is left us, for our friendly hand they spurn,
We can only meet as foemen — sad, but resolute and stern.

Father, dash aside the tear-drop, let thy proud boy go his way;
Mother, twine thine arms about him, and bless thy son this day;
Sister, weep, but yet look proudly, 'tis a time to do or die;
Maiden, clasp thy lover tenderly, as he whispers thee good-by.

Onward, onward to the battle, who can doubt which side will win!
Right and might both guard our squadrons, and the steadfast heart within;
Shall the men who never quailed before now falter in the field?
Or the men who fought at Bunker Hill be ever made to yield?

Then bless our banner, God of hosts! watch o'er each starry fold,
'Tis freedom's standard, tried and proved on many a field of old;
And Thou, who long hast blessed us, now bless us yet again,
And crown our cause with victory, and keep our flag from stain.

H. E. T.

OUR COUNTRY'S FLAG ON GOD'S SACRED ALTARS.

Where altars to our Maker rise,
There let His standards greet the skies;
And to heaven's welcoming breezes fling
The banners of Our Lord, the King!

Where Freedom's armies guard the land,
Let her proud standard-bearers stand
O'er hill and plain, from shore to shore,
Float her blest symbols ever more!

God of the Saints! land of the free!
Let thy fair banners blended be!
And o'er heaven's sacred altars wave
The flag that guards the free and brave!

Thus blended shall to us be given
The love of home, of God, and heaven!
Thus, in our grateful hearts shall rise,
Hopes of a home beyond the skies!

Thus shall religion's sacred fire
The patriot's heart with zeal inspire;
Thus shall the patriot's gifts, in turn,
On blest religion's altars burn!

And love of God walk hand in hand
With love of man and native land!
Christ's kingdom then the earth will span,
With "peace on earth — good will to man!"

        J. W. TEMPLE.

PROUDLY IN GLORY FLOATING O'ER US.

We will rally round the flag, boys, we'll rally once again,
    Proudly in glory floating o'er us ;
Always gallantly defend on every battle plain,
    Proudly in glory floating o'er us.

    The old flag forever ! hurrah ! boys, hurrah !
    We stood by " Old Glory," it hasn't lost a star;
    We will rally 'round the flag, boys, we'll rally once again,
    Proudly in glory floating o'er us.

'Twas for it our heroes fought in the woeful war-days past,
    Proudly in glory floating o'er us ;
For it marched in summer's sun, for it stood thro' winter's blast,
    Proudly in glory floating o'er us.

'Twas a fearful sacrifice that was offered for it then,
    Proudly in glory floating o'er us ;
Of the noblest and the best of Columbia's worthy men,
    Proudly in glory floating o'er us.

And to-day we'll firmly pledge, boys, we'll rally round the gift,
    Proudly in glory floating o'er us ;
That our deeds be ever faithful humanity to lift,
    Proudly in glory floating o'er us.

                                          J. E. THORP.

CONFERENCE RESOLUTION REGARDING OUR COUNTRY'S FLAG.

"Resolved, That we, as a conference, do recommend that the American flag be placed in our churches and Sunday-schools as an emblem of our Christian civilization."

Resolution passed by the Central Illinois Conference of the Methodist Episcopal Church, September 30th, 1889.

OUR FLAG AND THE CROSS.

We do not teach our children sufficiently what is due the "Old Flag"—what it stands for. It is to our institutions what the cross is to the Christian religion.

COLONEL HEPBURN.

THE FLAG O'ER OUR SCHOOL-HOUSE IS FLOATING.

O'er our school-house the "Old Flag" in beauty is floating,
    Its stars are as white as the purest of snow;
While the blue field they cover, a true peace denoting,
    And valor-lit stripes with a radiance glow.

For that flag means a sacrifice — martyred ones dying
    And suff'ring to rescue our "Home of the Free"—
For the war years were fearful that kept the flag flying,
    And won the prosperity all of us see.

In the rooms of our school-house, when wearied eyes raising,
    The grand flag before us doth nightily cheer;
How it rests aching heads, at its symmetry gazing,
    To think of the deeds that have made it so dear.

In our hearts, too, we carry the bright flag of glory,
    Its battle-tried grandeur to cherish through life;
Ever true to our country, we'll cherish the story,
    How heroes have saved it from war's bitter strife.

OUR FLAG IN THE SCHOOL-ROOM.

If I had my way, I would hang the flag in every schoolroom, and attempt to impress upon all the supreme value of their inheritance.

HON. ANDREW S. DRAPER,

OUR GLORIOUS ENSIGN.

Oh, raise that glorious ensign high,
    And let the nation see
That flag for which our fathers fought
    To make our country free!

From every hill, in every vale,
    Where freemen tread the sod,
And from the spires where freemen meet
    For prayer and praise to God,
Unfurl the flag beneath but this,
    The cross of Calvary.

                      ANONYMOUS.

THE FLAG OVER OUR CHURCHES.

"Let the flag of our country wave from the spire of every church in the land, with nothing above it save the cross of Christ."
REV. E. A. ANDERSON, 1861.

THE STARS AND STRIPES.

There is now no nation which is not familiar with the stars and stripes. In the seaports of ancient China our star-spangled ensign is known as "the flower-flag," its brilliant dyes suggesting to the fanciful Chinese a ready figure of speech. So the wandering Americans are sometimes spoken of as the "flower-flag people." To millions of men in other lands it is an emblem of popular liberty and human rights. To us it now means more than ever. It means a flag saved from dishonor, a nation preserved from disunion. The good Lincoln used to say during the war, that though he saw the flag every day he never regarded it for a moment without emotion. To him it represented a republic in danger. So, to-day, as it floats in sunny splendor from numberless spires and spars, on land and sea, in pompous folds or in the tiny leaflet of the children, we may well regard it fondly as bringing back the wonderful history of a hundred years.

It glitters on the proudest frigate as it glittered first on the "Ranger" of Paul Jones. It floats peacefully from Maine to Alaska, and from the lakes to the gulf, as it waved amid shot and shell on the fields where the republic was born and our right to a national flag was established. We do well to cherish a sentiment of passionate devotion to the old flag. No star is blotted, no stripe erased. It is the glory of countless homes.

> And when the wanderer, lonely, friendless,
> In foreign harbors shall behold
> That flag unrolled,
> 'Twill be as a friendly hand
> Stretched out from his native land,
> Filling his heart with memories sweet and endless
> ANONYMOUS.

STAND BY THE FLAG.

Stand by the flag, the flag of freedom's pride!
    Stand by the flag your fathers fought to save!
Stand by the flag for which those heroes died!
    Stand by the flag, that it may forever wave!

Stand by the flag, the flag of hope to earth!
    Stand by the flag, its stripes with valor glow!
Stand by the flag, bright stars of priceless worth!
    Stand by the flag, all lands its victories know!

Stand by the flag, tell freedom's brightest story!
    Stand by the flag, it proudly floats above!
Stand by the flag, maintain its grandest glory!
    Stand by the flag, the dear old flag we love!

J. C. O. REDINGTON.

OUR STAR-SPANGLED EMBLEM.

Our star-spangled emblem of valor and glory,
   The beautiful flag proudly floating above,
Forever tell over the glorious grand story
   Of what the flag means that the loyal all love.
                       J. C. O. REDINGTON.

OUR FLAG AND THE UNION FOREVER.

We will stand by the Union forever,
    By the flag of the brave and the true,
By the glorious star-spangled banner,
    With its beautiful red, white, and blue.

Oh, its folds to the free air of heaven,
    By our fathers unfurled long ago,
Shall ne'er wave o'er America riven
    By the hand of a traitorous foe.

On the field, o'er the dead and the dying,
    Where the loud din of battle is rife,
See our emblem of liberty flying,
    Oh, its triumph is dearer than life.

Let us trust in the might of Jehovah,
    For the right with His might must prevail.
With the flag of the free floating over
    Our hosts, Oh, we never shall fail.

Three-times-three for the Union forever,
    Three-times-three for the brave and the true,
Three-times-three for the star-spangled banner,
    With its beautiful red, white, and blue.

    See it waving, waving, waving,
        'Tis freedom's emblem rare,
    See it waving, waving, waving,
        In glorious triumph there.

                REV. J. MATLOCK.

TELL THE GLAD TIDINGS.

Wave 'neath the azure, ye banners so bright!
Hymns of devotion and valor recite!
Tell to the world how our heroes have died,
Bearing your colors aloft in their pride.
Tell it by shore and by murmuring sea!
Tell it where manhood is noble and free!
Your prestige and grandeur no dark shadow mars —
Tell the glad tidings, ye stripes and ye stars.
                                    ANONYMOUS.

BLESSINGS ON OUR BANNER.

God bless the banner of the free,
    The flag our fathers gave;
May stars and stripes on land and sea
    In triumph ever wave!
Columbia's emblem of her might,
    "Old Glory" floats above;
We'll strike for God and for the right!
    Its every fold we love.

Forever waving in the skies,
    Each year with glory new,
Maintained by fearful sacrifice
    Of noble "boys in blue."
This land be freedom's dwelling-place
    Our flag shall ever bear —
May liberty to human race
    O'er earth spread everywhere.

The endless years of coming time
    Shall echo freedom's voice;
The pilgrim here from every clime
    May in that flag rejoice.
The stars and stripes shall ever teach,
    To all who 'neath it stand,
Free soil, free men, free faith, free speech,
    To all in freedom's land.

                J. C. O. REDINGTON.

THE MEANING OF OUR FLAG.

The flag for which our heroes fought, for which they died, is the symbol of all we are, of all we hope to be. It is the emblem of equal rights. It means free hands, free lips, self-government, and the sovereignty of the individual. It means that this continent has been dedicated to freedom. It means universal education — light for every mind, knowledge for every child. It means that the school-house is the fortress of liberty. It means that "governments derive their just powers from the governed;" that each man is accountable to and for the government; that responsibility goes hand in hand with liberty. It means that it is the duty of every citizen to bear his share of the public burden — to take part in the affairs of his town, his county, his state, and his country. It means that the ballot-box is the ark of the covenant; that the source of authority must not be poisoned. It means the perpetual right of peaceful revolution. It means that every citizen of the republic, native or naturalized, must be protected at home in every state, abroad in every land, on every sea. It means that all distinctions based on birth or blood have perished from our laws; that our government shall stand between labor and capital, between the weak and the strong, between the individual and the corporation, between want and wealth, and give and guarantee simple justice to each and all. It means that there shall be a legal remedy for every wrong. It means national hospitality — that we must welcome to our shores the exiles of the world, and that we may not drive them back. Some may be deformed by labor, dwarfed by hunger, broken in spirit, victims of tyranny and cast — in whose sad faces may be read the touching record of a weary life — and yet their children, born of liberty and love, will be symmetrical and fair, intelligent and free.

COLONEL R. G. INGERSOLL.

LET OUR FLAG FLOAT O'ER EACH.

 Let our flag float far and wide,
 O'er each hero, true and tried,
 O'er the graves of all who died
  At our country's call.
 For the flag those martyrs bled,
 Freely noblest blood was shed,
" For our native land!" they said,
" Sacrifice we all."

      ANONYMOUS.

THE UNITED STATES FLAG AT NORTH CAPE, NORWAY.

A party of Americans found themselves, on the Fourth of July, 1880, at North Cape, Norway. They arrived in a steamer at 11 o'clock P. M., July 3d, and at one minute after midnight guns were fired, the shrill whistle of the engine responded to the number of stars on the American flag, and loud cheers were given to usher in our nation's holiday. The party then ascended the almost perpendicular cliff — nine hundred feet high — and raised an American flag, made by the ladies of the party out of materials purchased at one of the Norwegian towns. It was certainly an extraordinary place for such a celebration, and the first time that a company of Americans ever celebrated the Fourth of July at such an hour and at such a latitude. The midnight sun shone upon the party all the time with dazzling brightness.

KEEP THE FLAG AT THE FRONT.

Plant now the flag, the dear old flag, out in the front again!
As in advance, 'mid fire and death, the flag was planted then;
And round it rallied, till they fell, Columbia's glorious men,
    Whose sacrifice the nation saved.

    Hurrah! hurrah! the same old flag to-day!
    Hurrah! hurrah! let none forget the way
    'Twas brought through fearful sacrifice, where deadly perils lay,
        When carried by the boys in blue.

In patriot love by every one the strength of nation lies,
And ceaseless loyalty to flag, kept free by sacrifice;
To Liberty that all be true, let daily pledges rise
    From all the youth of Columbia.

Let nothing rise with loyalty to ever interfere,
Let nothing false to country ever anywhere appear;
Let songs and deeds the truth impress, that all the world may hear,
    Our hearts are true to Liberty.

                      J. C. O. REDINGTON.

WRAP THE FLAG AROUND ME, BOYS.

Wrap the flag around me, boys,
    To die were far more sweet,
With freedom's starry emblem, boys,
    To be my winding sheet.
In life I loved to see it wave,
    And follow where it lead,
But now my eyes grow dim, my hands
    Would clasp its last bright shred.

I had thought to greet you, boys,
    On many a well worn field,
When to our starry banner, boys,
    The traitorous foe should yield;
But now, alas! I am denied
    My dearest earthly prayer,
You'll follow and you will meet the foe,
    But I shall not be there.

But though my body moulder, boys,
    My spirit will be free,
And every comrade's honor, boys,
    Will still be dear to me.
Then in the thick and bloody fight,
    Ne'er let your ardor lag,
For I'll be there, still hov'ring near,
    Above the dear old flag.

                P. STEWART TAYLOR.

Copyrighted by A. S. Barnes & Co.

HURRAH FOR THE FLAG.

There are many flags in many lands,
    There are flags of every hue,
But there is no flag, however grand,
    Like our red, white, and blue.

We should always love the stars and stripes,
    And we mean to be ever true
To this land of ours and the dear old flag,
    The red, the white, and blue.

Then hurrah for the flag, "Our Country's Flag,"
    Its stripes and bright stars, too;
There is no flag in any land
    Like our red, white, and blue.

                    Miss M. H. Howliston.

HURRAH FOR THE OLD FLAG.

Just after the terrible battle of the first Bull Run six men were found close together with seven of their legs needing immediate amputation. One by one they were gathered up and carried on an improvised stretcher to the surgeon's table. When Corporal Tanner's (afterward United States Pension Commissioner) turn came, he was rolled on to the short stretcher and lifted up to be borne away — but now came the moment of trial. The rude appliance was too short for his body, and lying face downward he looked under the stretcher and saw both of his mangled legs hanging down at the other end. Catching a sight of the prostrate comrades just left, he shouted with all his remaining strength, "Hurrah for the old flag."

ANONYMOUS.

THE CHILDREN'S SONG OF THE FLAG.

This is our flag, and may it wave
    Wide over land and sea!
Though others love a different flag,
    This is the flag for me.

And that's the flag for all our land,
    We will revére no other,
And he who loves this symbol fair
    Shall be to us a brother.

America's the land we love,
    Our broad, fair land so free;
And, school-mates, whereso'er I go,
    This is the flag for me.

These glorious stars and radiant stripes,
    With youthful joy I see;
May no rude hand its beauty mar,
    This is the flag for me.

                    ANONYMOUS.

PREFERRED DEATH TO SURRENDERING THE FLAG.

In the war of 1812, when Stonington was being bombarded by the British fleet, August 10th, 1814, the town was wholly defenseless, the supply of ammunition having given out, and at the mercy of the invaders, a timid citizen proposed a formal surrender by lowering the United States flag, which was flying over a one-gun eighteen-pound battery.

"No," shouted Captain Holmes, indignantly, "that flag shall never come down while I am alive!" And when the wind died away and it hung drooping from its staff, the brave Captain held it out on the point of a bayonet that the British might see it. In that position several shots passed through it, and a companion of Holmes' was held up on his shoulders while he nailed it to the staff.

By permission, from "A... H... ck"

THE AMERICAN FLAG IN OUR SCHOOLS.

Flag of our nation! Symbol true,
The clustered stars on field of blue,
And stripes, alternate red and white,
Combine to teach and hold the right
To live and be at liberty,
As we our happy peace can see —
And share the blessings God designed
Should be the portion of mankind.

Thou art a patron of the mind,
And all Columbia's children find
Free education, public schools
Unfettered by a tyrant's rules —
Where all, both rich and poor, obtain
Instruction on an equal plane —
Whence come the good men, wise and great,
To guard or hold the chair of state.

Let, then, each public school possess
The flag whose virtues we confess;
To teach our country's hope — the young
The sources whence our goodness sprung,
And ever keep before their eyes,
A token of the sacrifice
Offered by freemen, true and brave,
Our liberties to gain and save.

Columbia, take now the stand
In every school-house in the land;
And to our eager youth unfold
The story of those days of old,
When freemen gathered at the call
To struggle, bleed, in death to fall,
So that the banner of thy choice
Might wave to make the world rejoice.
J. C. O. REDINGTON.

THE FLAG OF THE CONSTELLATION.

Stars of the morn on our banner borne,
    With heaven's iris blended,
The hands of our sires mingled first those fires,
    And by us they'll be defended.

        Then hail the true, the red, white, and blue!
           The flag of the constellation ;
        It sails as it sailed, by our fathers hailed,
           O'er battles that made us a nation.

What hand so bold as to strike from its fold
    A star or stripe there bright'ning !
To him each star be a fiery Mars,
    Each stripe a terrible lightning.

Its meteor form shall outride the storm
    'Till the fiercest foes surrender ;
The storm gone by, it shall gild the sky,
    A rainbow of peace and of splendor.

Peace to the world, is our motto unfurled,
    Tho' we fear no field that's gory :
At home or abroad, fearing none but God,
    Our own pathway we're carving to glory.

                    T. BUCHANAN REID.

THE AMERICAN FLAG IN NASHVILLE, TENN.

The following extract from a letter on the joy of seeing the American flag in Nashville was written by a young lady in that city in the early part of the war:

"Rejoice with me, dear grandma! The glorious star-spangled banner of the United States is again floating above us! Oh, how we have hoped for, longed for, prayed for this joyous day! I am wild, crazed, almost, with delight. I am still fearful that I shall awake and find our deliverance, our freedom, is all a dream. I cannot believe that it is a positive fact, it has come upon us so unexpectedly, this successful move of the Union army. Grandma, I cannot write connectedly at all. Forgive me all faults of composition, for I can see the stars and stripes of my ever-loved floating from the State House — the first time my eyes have been gladdened by such a sight for nearly a year. So great is my ecstasy, I cannot sit still. I cannot keep my eyes on the paper; indeed, I cannot do anything but sing, whistle, and hum 'Yankee Doodle,' 'Hail Columbia,' 'The Star-Spangled Banner,' and feast my eyes on those glorious colors. Oh, grandma! you cannot imagine our happiness at this sudden change in the aspect of public affairs. We have had so much to bear since I wrote you.

"My father and brother have been taunted, sneered, and hissed at, and threatened by every one, until endurance was becoming impossible. We have been warned that there was imminent danger here for them, and the hatred toward Union men was becoming so intense that both ma and I have been in an agony of suspense. We could not leave home, as we never did, without being insulted. The cloud was lowering over us, growing darker and darker day by day, and I thought the silver lining never would appear, but it is here! even now beaming upon us so brightly that we can scarcely credit the reality. Can you wonder that in the state of feeling I was in that Sunday morning, dear grandma, when Tom knocked at the door and called out to me that Fort Donelson was surrendered, and the federal army would soon be in Nashville, I became perfectly frantic with joy? I ran screaming over the house, knocking down chairs and tables, clapping my hands, and shouting for the Union until the children were terrified, and ma and pa thought I was delirious. I rushed into the parlor and thundered 'Yankee Doodle' on the piano in such a manner as I had never done before. I caught little Johnnie up in my arms and held him over the porch railing up stairs until he hurrahed for the star-spangled banner, Seward, Lincoln, and McClellan. Just in the midst of these rejoicings intelligence came that Johnston's army was fleeing along the turnpike. Yes, there they were, retreating most 'valiantly.' Grandma, you never saw such a set of frightened men; they could not get over the river fast enough. I never bade the southern army 'God-speed' but that once, and then I did it with my whole heart. May their present advance be successful even to the Gulf of Mexico itself!"

OH, WRAP ME IN THE FLAG.

Oh, wrap me in the flag, boys,
    When I am called to rest.
We've fought beneath that banner
    That millions might be blest;
We've borne that sacred standard
    On many a fiery field,
And counted it, from heaven,
    Our country's holy shield.

Around me fold the flag, boys,
    When ready for my grave,
So we may sleep with comrades
    Who died the stars to save.
We battled as true brothers
    To keep the right on high,
Then let us sleep together
    Where freedom's heroes lie.

Yes, wrap the star-flag o'er me,
    That I may rest with braves;
We're sure the stars above us
    Will lumine all our graves.
Our nation's peerless colors
    Were borrowed from the skies—
A cheer to dying martyrs,
    And dear to angel eyes.

No flag among the nations
  With ours may be compared;
No banner in earth's conflicts
  Has equal glory shared.
Before it despots tremble,
  Tyrants are filled with awe;
It breathes full inspiration
    Of liberty and law.
        COMRADE CHAPLAIN E. DENNISON

LET US HAVE PEACE.

A quarter of a century has passed since the great commander of the Union army received the surrender of Lee at Appomattox, and as he stretched his hand out to take the hand of Lee, he said to him and to a weary nation tired of war: "Let us have peace." And we wish peace from one end of the land to the other; and we wish at the same time to see the flag we love revered wherever it floats. We hope, too, the time is not far distant when it will be floating from every school-house in the land. We wish to see it enshrined in the hearts and in the homes of every man, woman, and child in this great nation, even as the shadow of the cross of the Savior is enshrined in the heart of the believer.

GENERAL R. A. ALGER,
Commander-in-Chief of G. A. R.

[From the "Toledo Blade," July 1, 1870.]

THE FLAG'S COME BACK TO TENNESSEE.

" Move my arm chair, faithful Pompey,
    In the sunlight, clear and strong;
For this world is fading, Pompey,
    Massa won't be with you long;
And I fain would hear the south wind
    Bring once more the sound to me
Of the wavelets softly breaking
    On the shores of Tennessee.

" Mournful, though, the ripples murmur,
    As they still the story tell
How no vessels float the banner
    That I've loved so long and well.
I shall listen to their music,
    Dreaming that again I see
Stars and stripes on sloop and shallop,
    Sailing up the Tennessee."

Thus he watches cloud bow shadows
    Glide from tree to mountain crest,
Softly creeping, aye, and ever,
    To the river's yielding breast.
Ha! above the foliage yonder
    Something flutters, bold and free —
" Massa, massa, hallelujah!
    The flag's come back to Tennessee!"

" Pompey, hold me on your shoulder,
　　Help me stand on foot once more,
That I may salute the colors
　　As they pass my cabin door.
Never more shall treason trail thee,
　　Glorious emblem of the free!
God and Union be our watchword
　　Evermore in Tennessee!"

NO DESECRATION OF "OLD GLORY."

Congressman Caldwell, of Cincinnati, has become known as the champion of the American flag. The house, on Monday, September 29th, 1890, passed his bill to protect the flag from "defacement, disfigurement, or prostitution to the purposes of advertising."

OUR BANNER OF GLORY.

Our banner of glory is waving on high,
    Its stars are as those of the even',
And its stripes like the mingling hues of the sky
    When the morning is blushing in heaven.

That banner, still radiant and floating on high,
    From ocean to ocean still reigning,
Shall illumine the sea and rival the sky
    While an empire on earth is remaining.

Wave on! then, wave on, thou flag of the free!
    Be never defeated, no, never!
Triumphantly wave o'er land and the sea!
    Proudly wave in thy glory forever!

                  J. C. O. REDINGTON.

"Our banner of glory _____
Its stars are as those of the _____"

A LOVELY BANNER.

Ne'er waved beneath the golden sun
    A lovelier banner for the brave,
Than that our bleeding fathers won,
    And proudly to their children gave.

Its glorious stars in azure shine,
    The radiant heraldry of heaven;
Its stripes in beauteous order twine,
    The emblems of our Union given.

Around the globe, through every clime
    Where commerce wafts or man hath trod,
It floats aloft, unstained with crime,
    But hallowed by heroic blood.

                      ANONYMOUS.

[From "The Flag of the United States."]

THE NATIONAL FLAG.

There is the national flag! He must be cold, indeed, who can look upon its folds rippling in the breeze without pride of country. If he be in a foreign land, the flag is companionship and country itself, with all its endearments. Who, as he sees it, can think of a state merely? Whose eye, once fastened upon its radiant trophies, can fail to recognize the image of the whole nation? It has been called a floating piece of poetry; and yet I know not if it have any intrinsic beauty beyond other ensigns. Its highest beauty is in what it symbolizes. It is because it represents all that all gaze at it with delight and reverence. It is a piece of bunting lifted in the air; but it speaks sublimely, and every part has a voice. Its stripes of alternate red and white proclaim the original union of thirteen states to maintain the Declaration of Independence. Its stars, white in a field of blue, proclaim that union of states constituting our national constellation, which receives a new star with every new state. The two together signify union, past and present. The very colors have a language which was officially recognized by our fathers. White is for purity, red for valor, blue for justice; and all together — bunting, stripes, stars, and colors, blazing in the sky — make the flag of our country; to be cherished by all hearts, to be upheld by all our hands.

Hon. CHARLES SUMNER.

COLORS THAT WILL NOT RUN.

When the people of the north were excited on the fall of Fort Sumter, a New York sign-painter hung out the stars and stripes with the significant statement that they were "colors warranted not to run."

OUR COUNTRY'S FLAG IN THE WHITE HOUSE.

One of the flags in the White House has a history with which few are familiar. It hangs over the center of the largest window of the east room, where it can be seen to the best advantage. It is woven of silk in one heavy piece. There is no seam in it. Amid the gold stars appears on the field, in French:

"Popular subscription to the Republic of the United States. Offered in memory of Abraham Lincoln, Lyons, 1865."

FLAG OF GLORY.

Onward, flag of glory, flying,
Higher rise to fame undying;
Borne aloft by freedom now,
Grandest earthly banner, thou.
Thine, oh, stars and stripes, the story
Of a nation's wondrous glory,
Won from field and conflict gory,
Symbol of its power and worth.

      J. D. PHELPS.

MY FATHER'S FLAG AND MINE.

Oh! that grand old flag of glory
    That our veteran fathers bore
While the loyal hosts were struggling
    Through the crimson storms of war!
On the fiery front of battle,
    See it flash along the line!
'Tis the old "Star-Spangled Banner" —
    My father's flag and mine.

    Oh, the beauty! oh, the glory!
        That in radiant splendor shine
    In the old "Star-Spangled Banner" —
        My father's flag and mine.

There were many millions lying
    'Neath the tyrants crushing might,
And their blood to heaven was crying
    Through that long and tearful night —
'Till they caught the light of freedom,
    With its radiance divine,
From the old "Star-Spangled Banner" —
    My father's flag and mine.

Oh! the blood, the tears, the agonies
    It in every fibre holds!
Oh! the grand heroic spirits —
    We see them in its folds!
'Tis the ensign of the ages!
    It is freedom's gift and shrine!
That dear old "Star-Spangled Banner" —
    My father's flag and mine.

SONS OF VETERANS AND OUR FLAG.

Sons of Veterans, take the colors,
    Never lower the silken bars;
Ever be a band of brothers,
    Rallying 'round the stripes and stars.
Sons of Veterans, we are growing
    Fewer, fewer year by year;
Thick the graves with colors flowing,
    Yellow is the leaf, and sear.
Swear to keep this banner flying,
    Tho' foreign foe or traitor's band
Should strew the fields with dead and dying,
    And other flags pollute the land.
Sons of Veterans, you are given
    That which all our hearts revere;
Though it should be rent and riven,
    It will conquer, never fear.

                COLONEL J. H. PIERCE.

THE PATRIOT'S FLAG.

The true American patriot is ever a worshipper. The starry symbol of his country's sovereignty is to him radiant with a diviner glory than that which meets his mortal vision. It epitomizes the splendid results of dreary ages and failures in human government, and as he gazes upon its starry folds undulating to the whispering winds of the upper air, it sometimes seems to his enraptured spirit to recede further and further into the soft blue skies until the heavens open and angel hands plant it upon the battlements of paradise. Its stars seem real; its lines of white symbol the purity of his heroic sires, those of red their patriot blood shed in defense of right. To insult that flag is worse than infamy; to make war upon it worse than treason. Where that ensign floats, on the sea or on the land, it is to him the very political shekinah of his love and faith, luminous with the presence of that God who conducted our fathers across the sea and through the fires of the revolution to the Pisgah heights of civil and religious liberty.

NEWTON BATEMAN.

OUR BANNER!

For fifty years, at fray or feast,
O'er deadly foe or gentle guest,
   Triumphantly unfurled!
And fifty more our flag shall wave
In memory of the good and brave
   Who dignified the world,
And tyranny and time defy
In freedom's immortality.

THE GLORIOUS ENSIGN.

" Oh, raise that glorious ensign high,
    And let the nations see
The flag for which our fathers fought
    To make our country free ! "

                              ANONYMOUS.

OUR BANNER OF LIGHT.

"Hail, banner of glory! Hail, banner of light!
Whose fame lives in story, whose folds cheer my sight;
Not a star is suppres'd, not a stripe has been torn
From the flag of the West, which our fathers have borne.
Our Union is fast, and our homes ever sure,
Our freedom shall last while the world shall endure.
Then hail to the banner whose folds wave in glory,
Let the free breezes fan her and whisper her story —
The tumult has ended, the storm's died away,
The fiend has descended that led us astray ;
The sons of the West are our brothers again,
And the flag of the blest floats from Texas to Maine."

J. C. S.

THE UNITED STATES FLAG IN BATTLE.

During the war of the great rebellion the United States flag waved in the smoke of 2,247 battles, and 2,690,401 men mustered under its folds.

OUR HONORED FLAG.

"A stretch of bunting floating o'er
    Our heads — red stripes, on ground of white
    A blue space, like the sky at night —
Some stars in clusters — nothing more!

"Why wave your hats? Why shout with joy?
    Why flaunt this picture to the breeze?
    An artist's eye 'twill fail to please,
This flaring gaud — this painted toy!"

"Stranger! thou read'st its legend ill!
    That canvas, wrestling with the winds,
    Holds a deep meaning for our minds,
Passing the artist's boasted skill!

"That ground of white is Time's vast page —
    Those tell-tale lines of deepest red
    The blood by martyr-patriots shed
In every clime, through every age!

"That bright, clear space of azure hue
    That hides apart from all the rest,
    Means our fair empire of the west,
Whose sky of hope is ever blue!

"Those stars that deck night's ample breast
    Shall glitter on through countless years —
    While gravitation rules the spheres
Each orb draws closer all the rest!

"See, stranger! in yon flag, unfurled,
    Life's highest aim, time's weightiest trust!
    For when that banner trails in dust
Freedom, faith, hope will leave the world!"

                  JAMES W. TEMPLE.

JAMES A. GARFIELD AND OUR FLAG.

"I trust the time is not far distant when in the North and South our people will sleep in peace and rise in liberty, love, and harmony under the union of our flag of the stars and stripes."

OUR GLORIOUS FLAG.

Oh, glorious flag! red, white, and blue,
Bright emblem of the pure and true;
Oh, glorious group of clustering stars!
Ye lines of light, ye crimson bars,
Trampled in dust by traitor feet,
Once more your flowing folds we greet
Triumphant over all defeat;
Henceforth in every clime to be,
Unfading scarf of liberty,
The ensign of the brave and free.

HON. EDWARD J. PRESTON.

FLAG OF MY COUNTRY

Flag of my country! in thy folds
    Are wrapped the treasures of the heart;
Where'er that waving sheet is fanned
By breezes of the sea and land,
    It bids the life-blood start.

It is not that among those stars
    The firey crest of Mars shines out;
It is not that on battle-plain,
'Mid heaps of harnessed warriors slain,
    It flaps triumphant o'er the route.

Short-lived the joy that conquest yields;
    Flushed victory is bathed in tears;
The burden of that bloody fame
Which shouting myriads proclaim
    Sounds sad to widowed ears.

Thou hast a deeper, stronger hold,
    Flag of my country, on the heart —
That when o'er mustered hosts unfurled
Thou art a signal to the world
    At which the nations start.

Thou art a symbol of the power
    Whose sheltering wings our homes surround;
Guarded by thee was childhood's morn,
And where thy cheering folds are borne
    Order and peace are found.

Flag of our mighty Union, hail!
    Blessings abound where thou dost float;
Best robe for living freedom's form,
Fit pall to spread upon her tomb
    Should heaven to death devote.

Wave over us in glory still,
    And be our guardian as now!
Each wind of heaven salute thy streaks!
And withered be the arm that seeks
    To bring that banner low!
WILLIAM PARSONS LUNT.

DEDICATION OF A UNITED STATES FLAG SENT BY LADIES OF NEW YORK TO THE SEVENTH REGIMENT.

The flag of our country; what higher assurance
    Of sympathy, honor, and trust could we send?
The crown of our father's unflinching endurance,
    'Tis the emblem of all you have sworn to defend;
Of freedom and progress, with order combined,
    The cause of the nation, of God, and mankind.
                             ANONYMOUS.

OUR FLAG IS THERE.

Our flag is there, our flag is there,
    We'll hail it with three loud huzzas.
Our flag is there, our flag is there,
    Behold the glorious stripes and stars.
Stout hearts have fought for that bright flag,
    Strong hands upheld it mast-head high,
And oh! to see how proud it waves
    Brings tears of joy to every eye.

    Our flag is there, our flag is there,
        We'll hail it with three loud huzzas.
    Our flag is there, our flag is there,
        Behold the glorious stripes and stars.

That flag has stood the battle's roar,
    With foemen stout, with foemen brave;
Strong hands have sought that flag to lower,
    And found a sure and speedy grave.
That flag is known on every shore,
    The standard of a gallant band,
Alike unstained in peace and war,
    It floats o'er freedom's happy land.

        By a Naval Officer in 1812.

THE FLAG RESTORED.

General Sherman, on his march to join General Grant, captured Charleston, S. C., and on April 14th, 1865, the identical Union flag which had been hauled down at the surrender of Fort Sumter, exactly four years before, was finally restored with befitting ceremonies.

The multitude assembled and sang, "Rally 'Round the Flag." Rev. Mr. Harris, who made the prayer at the raising of the flag over Fort Sumter, December 27th, 1860, offered prayer, and pronounced a blessing on the flag. General Townsend read Major Anderson's dispatch announcing the fall of Sumter. Then faithful Sergeant Hart appeared with a carpet-bag containing the identical old flag, and General Anderson, after a brief and touching address, hoisted it to the peak of the flag-staff amid loud huzzahs, followed by singing "The Star-Spangled Banner." Six guns on the old fort were then fired and were responded to by all the batteries that took part in the bombardment, April 14th, 1861.

[From "Political Poetry."]

E PLURIBUS UNUM.

Though many and bright are the stars that appear
    In that flag by our country unfurled,
And the stripes that are swelling in majesty there,
    Like a rainbow adorning the world,
Their light is unsullied as those in the sky,
    By a deed that our fathers have done,
And they are linked in as true and as holy a tie,
    In their motto of "Many in One."

From the hour when those patriots fearlessly flung
    That banner of starlight abroad,
Ever true to themselves, to that motto they clung,
    As they clung to the promise of God.
By the bayonet traced at the midnight of war,
    On the field where our glory was won —
Oh, perish the heart or the hand that would mar
    Our motto of "Many in One."

'Mid the smoke of the conflict, the cannon's deep roar,
    How oft it has gathered renown!
While those stars were reflected in rivers of gore,
    Where the cross and the lion went down;
And though few were their lights in the gloom of that hour,
    Yet the hearts that were striking below
Had God for their bulwark, and truth for their power,
    And they stopped not to number their foe.

From where our green mountain-tops blend with the sky,
    And the giant St. Lawrence is rolled,
To the waves where the balmy Hesperides lie,
    Like the dream of some prophet of old.
They conquered, and, dying, bequeathed to our care
    Not their boundless dominion alone,
But that banner whose loveliness hallows the air,
    And their motto of "Many in One."

We are many in one while glitters a star
    In the blue of the heavens above,
And tyrants shall quail, 'mid their dungeons afar,
    When they gaze on that motto of love.
It shall gleam o'er the sea, 'mid the bolts of the storm,
    Over tempest, and battle, and wreck,
And flame where our guns with their thunder grow warm,
    'Neath the blood of the slippery deck.

The oppressed of the earth to that standard shall fly
    Wherever its folds shall be spread,
And the exile shall feel 'tis his own native sky,
    Where its stars shall wave over his head;
And those stars shall increase 'till the fullness of time
    Its millions of cycles have run —
'Till the world shall have welcomed their mission sublime,
    And the nations of earth shall be one.

Though the old Allegheny may tower to heaven,
    And the Father of Waters divide,
The links of our destiny cannot be riven
    While the truth of those words shall abide.
Oh, then let them glow on each helmet and brand,
    Though our blood like our rivers shall run;
Divide as we may in our own native land,
    To the rest of the world we are ONE.

Then up with our flag! Let it stream on the air;
    Though our fathers are cold in their graves,
They had hands that could strike, they had souls that could dare,
    And their sons were not born to be slaves.
Up, up with that banner! where'er it may call,
    Our millions shall rally around,
And a nation of freemen that moment shall fall
    When its stars shall be trailed on the ground.
GEORGE WASHINGTON CUTTER.

A LESSON TO BE TAUGHT IN OUR PUBLIC SCHOOLS.

The following extract is taken from a speech delivered by Dr. Richard Edwards, Illinois State Superintendent of Public Instruction, 1890:

"One of the lessons to be taught in these schools is the lesson of patriotism. Let the flag wave over every schoolhouse. Let the children within its walls be instructed in the principles of patriotism. Let them recite the poems which set forth the glories of our land. Let them declaim the speeches which proclaim the true principles of its government. Let them learn what the fathers of the republic said. Let them learn the great and inspiring facts in the nation's history. And let them revere the flag. It is the symbol of their country's greatness. It reminds you of the glories of the revolutionary war. It reminds you of the fact that in the greatest civil contest that was ever waged on earth this nation came out victor. Its power and its grandeur are to-day represented by the stars and stripes. Let the children read in the RED of the flag the story of the precious blood that has been shed in defense of the nation's liberties and the nation's existence. Let them discern in its glorious BLUE the purity of the principles on which it is founded, the heavenly, the inspiring sentiments which have animated her sons and daughters in all trying times. And let them read in the WHITE the lofty purity of those principles, their tendency to uplift and cleanse humanity, their mighty influence in regenerating the race."

[From "A...me H...v...ck, ...]

OUR FLAG, OUR PRIDE.

Our pride and cheer is our flag so dear,
    Our stars and stripes all glorious;
For far and near all the nations hear
    That it always is victorious.

        Let us all renew to the red, white, and blue
            Full measure of devotion;
        Ever shall it wave o'er our land of the brave,
            All free to the farthest ocean.

Once England rose, as the proudest of foes,
    With her navy to crush our nation;
But true hist'ry shows Yankee pluck that opposed
    Was the best in the whole creation.

The reason, you see, is our men are free;
    This fact ev'ry heart is firing;
And so mightily it will always be
    Invincible, inspiring.

Flag of the free! evermore to be
    Triumphant in its glory;
How, as queen of the sea, it has made foes flee,
    Is the grandest of all earth's story.

Our people, too, now are wholly true
    To the flag so well defended;
We are all true blue, loyal through and through,
    Civil war is forever ended.

                      J. C. O. REDINGTON.

THE FLAG OF SUMTER AND FINAL UNION.

Oh, see you our flag in the breeze floating bright
    On the walls of Fort Sumter, as the day is declining?
How proudly it waves as its stripes catch the light!
    What a glory of stars in its azure is shining!

There was woe in the land for the loss of brave men
Ere the flag o'er that fort was seen flying again;
But thence came a Union more firm than before,
One nation for aye, and one flag evermore!

ANONYMOUS.

A FLAG OF 1776 AT THE CENTENNIAL, 1876.

At the Centennial exhibition at Philadelphia in 1876 a reproduction of the Union flag raised at Cambridge in 1776 was hoisted over the old State House, January 1st, 1876.

THE HALLOWED FLAG.

Our flag, more than one hundred years
    Unfurled 'mid storm and sun —
The flag the tyrant hates and fears,
    Shall ne'er be undone.
Stand by the flag while life remains,
    For it man every gun ;
Beneath its folds, on battle-plains,
    Our Union grand was won.

    From sire to son, the flag hand down,
        And follow where it waves ;
    Unsullied be its fair renown,
        Hallowed our heroes' graves.

God bless our flag of stripes and stars,
    Proud symbol of the free ;
No stain its dazzling record mars,
    Honored on land and sea.
From eastern wave to western strand,
    Forever may it be
Emblem of freedom pure and grand,
    Symbol of liberty.

We'll ne'er give up our flag of fame,
    God speed its onward way ;
Dishonored be the hand and name
    That e'er disowns its sway.
Beneath the starry banner's sweep,
    Waiting the judgment day,
Four hundred thousand heroes sleep,
    Who fell before the gray.

Holy with memories pure and grand,
    Baptized with blood and tears,
Triumphant o'er our rescued land,
    Wave on a thousand years.
True patriots all would dare to die
    Where bright our flag appears;
And prouder yet 'twill kiss the sky,
    After a thousand years.
Prof. J. Howard Wert.

BRAVE WORDS.

"Lay me down, and save the flag."
              COLONEL JAMES MULLIGAN.

From "A mo H..." ...

THE FLAG WITH FORTY-TWO STARS.

Of all the mighty nations in the east or in the west,
Columbia is the grandest and the free-est and the best;
Her sacrifice for liberty astounded all the world,
And taught the wondrous meaning of the stars and stripes
    unfurled.

> Then cheer the flag! Glorious flag! flag of the free!
> Let us all to-day renew our loyalty!
> Only thirteen stars at first appeared to view,
> But now the mighty banner proudly carries forty-two.

A quarter-century has passed, of progress wondrous, grand,
And valiant deeds have made us now at head of nations stand;
All heed the people's uttered will, in grand, resistless vow,
We love "Old Glory" more and more, and we'll stand by it
    now,

Now let ev'ry happy one remember what our land has cost,
How for Union's preservation many noblest lives were lost;
And pledge anew to liberty an earnest, loyal heart,
That ev'ry day, both young and old, we'll do a patriot's part.

J. C. O. REDINGTON.

EXTRACT FROM HONORABLE EDWARD EVERETT'S ELOQUENT SPEECH AT A FLAG-RAISING IN BOSTON, 1861.

"We set up this standard," he said, "not as a matter of display, but as an expressive vindication that in the mighty struggle which has been forced upon us we are of one heart and mind — that the government of the country must be sustained." * * * * "Why is it," he continued, "that the flag of the country, always honored, always beloved, is now at once worshipped, I may say, with the passionate homage of this whole people? Why does it float, as never before, not merely from arsenal and mast-head, but from tower and steeple, from public edifices, the temples of science, the private dwellings, in magnificent display of miniature presentment? Let Fort Sumter give the answer. When on this day fortnight, the 13th of April (a day forever to be held in auspicious remembrance, like the dies Alliensis in the annals of Rome), the tidings spread through the land that the standard of united America, the pledge of her union and the symbol of her power, for which so many gallant hearts had poured out their life's blood on the ocean and the land to uphold, had, in the harbor of Charleston, been for a day and a half the target of eleven fratricidal batteries, one deep, unanimous, spontaneous feeling shot with the tidings through the breasts of twenty millions of freemen that its outraged honor must be vindicated."

FLAG OF YANKEE DOODLE.

In those old days of seventy-six
    There was a great commotion;
When Johnny Bull thought he would fix
    Things here more to his notion.
He said it was a stupid rag
    The Yankees were a-flying;
But Yankee Doodle said, "That flag
    Was never made for dying!"

    Yankee Doodle's glorious flag,
        Yankee Doodle Dandy,
    Floats from freedom's vict'ry crag,
        Old Yankee Doodle Dandy!

Some other fellows thought they'd try
    This flag to pull to pieces;
They found it vain, so said "good-bye!
    With us disunion ceases."
Our boys struck back with victor's whack
    And said, "This flag we're saving!
The Yankee Jack has got a knack
    Of keeping up a waving."

                    ANONYMOUS.

[From "The Flag of the United States," by P.   ]

SAVED BY SINGING THE STAR-SPANGLED BANNER.

After the battle of Belmont a wounded man, with both legs nearly shot off, was found in the woods singing the "Star-Spangled Banner;" but for this circumstance the surgeons say they would not have discovered him.

THE BANNER OF THE UNION.

Bring the good old banner, boys, the flag our fathers bore!
Let it float across the land and shimmer on the shore.
Liberty is marching on to many conquests more,
Bearing the banner of the Union.

>Hurrah! hurrah! we'll bring the jubilee;
>Hurrah! hurrah! the flag that makes us free;
>So we'll sing the chorus of truth and liberty,
>Bearing the banner of the Union.

How the nation thundered when that flag was menaced long;
How the boys enlisted and the girls grew bold and strong;
How the hosts of victory triumphant swept along,
Bearing the banner of the Union.

Rally 'round the colors, boys, and keep them at the fore,
Take your stand for liberty and fight her battles o'er,
True to home and freedom, ever loyal to the core,
Bearing the banner of the Union.

KATE BROWNLEE SHERWOOD.

From "History of the United St..." [...]

ITALIANS HONORING OUR FLAG.

In May, 1848, when the Italian tri-colored banner was consecrated by the Patriarch of Venice, in that city, the American consul was the only foreign diplomat invited to be present. In the course of the ceremonies the commander of the troops called, "Attention! Honor the flag of the United States of America!" At which the multitude shouted their applause with cries of "Long live our sister republic!" The people of all classes and conditions, soldiers and civilians, nearest, embraced the consul, and kissed the star-spangled banner, pressed it to their hearts, while the many, with moistened eyes, reached their hats through the crowd merely to touch it, exclaiming, "Viva il Console!" "Vivano gli Stati Uniti!" "Viva la gran Republica!"

THE HERALDRY OF THE AMERICAN FLAG.

When kingly presumption loosed war's desolation,
    To sweep o'er Columbia and sully her charms,
Our fathers united to form us a nation,
    And symboled it well in our blazon of arms.
Their homes were thirteen, so they followed that number —
    Seven red and six white, in a series of bars;
And, painting love's vigilance, foreign to slumber —
    They chose a blue quarter with thirteen white stars.

Thirteen blazed at once in their new constellation,
    The daughters of freedom, a star for each mate;
A new silver star is the fine augmentation
    Of honor they granted for every new state.
They named no abatement in view of secession,
    But bound us, their children, to foster the trust.

The white of the field proved their hate of oppression,
    Their passion for peace and abhorrence of war;
The red, in excess, warned o'erweening aggression
    It aye should be met and repulsed from their shore.
Truth shines in the quarter thus tinctured of heaven;
    Youth and strength light the stars that have ne'er paled
        or set.
Year by year they increase — may God grant that their levin,
    Extending, shall re-youth the continents yet.

So fashioned our fathers the flag of the Union,
    Which glads every wave of the world-lashing sea —
Revered by each man in our patriot communion —
    The handsomest banner that rides on the breeze.
With this sign they conquered. 'Midst cannon and mortar,
    Sword, musket, and rifle, still glitters this shield;
A people who stoop to no nation for quarter,
    A field present ever where foes are afraid.

As the stars and the stripes are our states interwoven,
    Having grown thus from weakness to far-spreading might,
Then perish the villain who, wanting them cloven,
    Would quench their resplendence in treachery's night!

CHARLES J. LUKENS.

THE COLORS IN OUR FLAG — WHAT THEY REPRESENT.

The red, white, and blue in the United States flag represent courage, integrity, steadfastness, love, and purpose.

FREEDOM'S FLAG.

Our country's flag, oh, emblem dear
　　Of all the soul loves best!
What glory in thy folds appear
　　Let noble deeds attest;
Thy presence on the field of strife
　　Enkindles valor's flame;
Around thee in the hour of peace
　　We twine our nation's fame.

Beneath thy rays our fathers bled
　　In freedom's holy cause;
Where'er to heaven thy folds outspread,
　　Prevail sweet freedom's laws.
Prosperity has marked thy course
　　O'er all the land and sea,
Thy favored sons in distant climes
　　Still fondly look to thee.

Proud banner of the noble free,
　　Emblazoned from on high!
Long may thy folds unsoiled reflect
　　The glories of the sky!
Long may thy land be freedom's land,
　　Thy homes with virtue bright,
Thy sons a brave, united band,
　　For God, for truth, and right!

　　Then hurrah! hurrah! for freedom's flag,
　　　　We hail with ringing cheers
　　Its glowing bars and clustering stars,
　　　　That have braved a hundred years.
　　　　　　　　　　　　GIEBEL.

THE FLAG AND THE UNION.

We join ourselves to no party that does not carry the flag and keep step to the music of the Union.

RUFUS CHOATE.

THE FIRST UNION FLAG OVER THE CAPITOL OF THE CONFEDERACY AFTER THE SURRENDER.

The first Union flag hoisted over the Capitol of the Confederacy upon the surrender of Richmond, Virginia, was the garrison flag of the Twelfth Maine Regiment, and had floated over the St. Charles hotel, New Orleans, when that building was General Butler's headquarters. It had been brought to Virginia by General Shepley, who hoped to raise it over the surrendered city of Richmond, also. He gave it in charge of Lieutenant Johnston L. De Peyster, a young man eighteen years of age, and a member of General Weitzel's staff. The young Lieutenant carried the flag on the pummel of his saddle for several days, expecting daily to take part in the assault upon the city. On April 3d, 1865, at about 8:30 o'clock in the morning, he, assisted by Captain Loomis L. Langdon, of General Weitzel's staff, raised the historic banner over the captured Capitol of the Confederacy.

OUR STAR-SPANGLED BANNER FOREVER.

We sing of the Union, the Union we love,
    The Union that nothing shall sever.
We sing of our banner, free, floating above;
    Undimmed may it wave on forever!

    Serene 'mid the nations Columbia stands,
        United, unrivalled as ever;
    Our Union of states, of hearts, and of hands,
        And our star-spangled banner forever!

We sing of our Union made perfect again —
    Our Union all rupture defying;
We sing of our flag, on the land, o'er main,
    Triumphant o'er head it is flying.

We sing of our Union, our Union renewed,
    Cemented more firmly than ever.
We sing of the flag loyal blood has imbued —
    A star shall be torn from it never!

We sing of the Union we live in to-day,
    The stronger since its recent saving.
The "Yank" of the blue, and the "Johnny" of gray
    Both are glad the old flag is waving.

In letters of gold on fame's scroll shall appear
    To all future ages the story.
Three cheers for the Union, our Union so dear,
    Three cheers for our star-flag, "Old Glory!"

                NELLIE GRISWOLD JOHNSON.

MONEY BEQUEATHED FOR FLAGS.

Soon after the close of the war Jacob Foss, a citizen of Charlestown, Massachusetts, bequeathed to that city several thousand dollars, the interest to be expended in United States flags. No mottoes are to be emblazoned on these flags, nor are they to be used for party purposes; but on all important occasions of a national character they are to be hoisted to the breeze and kept flying.

ALL ONE UNDER THE STARS AND STRIPES.

So, under one banner united,
    Though natives of different lands,
Our faith to our country is plighted.
    We give it our hearts and our hands.
A Union that time shall not sever,
    Whose pledges to-day we renew,
The star-spangled banner forever!
    Three cheers for the red, white, and blue.

ANONYMOUS.

[From the Century Magazine.]

A MONOPOLY OF THE FLAG.

It is the right of the American people to enjoy a monopoly for their own flag within their own jurisdiction; it is the right, and should be the duty, of those who follow other flags to follow them elsewhere.

YES! OUR FLAG IS STILL ADVANCING.

Is "our banner" still advancing?
    Hear the loyal hosts exclaim,
While the rallying ranks of freedom
    Onward dash, 'mid smoke and flame.
Onward up the fort-ribbed mountain,
    'Gainst the leaden storm they passed,
'Till the grand old flag of freedom
    Waved in triumph o'er its crest!

Yes! Our flag is still advancing!
    See! It mounts toward the sun!
Rebel legions dash against it,
    But it still keeps moving on!
Traitors aim their deadly missiles,
    Monarchs frown across the main,
But the foe of human freedom
    Aims and frowns and strikes in vain!

Is "our banner" still advancing?
    Gasped the soldier as he died,
While the blood his heart was yielding
    Trickled down the mountain side.
But his comrades hurried onward,
    'Till the mountain top they trod!
They have scaled that dreaded mountain,
    He has scaled the "mount of God!"

Yes! "Our flag" is still advancing!
    As yon radiant orb of day,
Mounting to its heavenly zenith,
    Makes the shadows fade away —
So "our flag" dispels oppression;
    Lo! 'Tis freedom's rising sun,
Earth's last fetter shall be broken,
    E'er its radiant race is run.

Is "our banner" still advancing?
    Rings the echo through the air;
Well may freemen swell that chorus,
    All their hopes are centered there.
Bear aloft that grand "old banner,"
    While our rallying hosts repeat:
"This shall be our nation's glory,
    Or our nation's winding sheet!"

Yes! "Our flag" is still advancing!
    How these words our bosoms thrill!
May our sons in coming ages
    Keep that flag advancing still —
'Till o'er all this vast dominion,
    Where the foot of man hath trod,
All shall bow 'neath freedom's banner,
    All shall worship freedom's God!

    Still advancing, higher! higher!
        Shout ye loyal! Shout ye brave!
    Tyrants, let your hope expire
        When you see that banner wave!
    Still advancing! Oh! we hail thee!
        In thy grandeur ever wave!
    Perish all who dare assail thee,
        Grand old banner of the brave!
                CHAPLAIN LOZIER.

STAND BY OUR COUNTRY'S FLAG.

Stand by the flag, its folds have streamed in glory,
    To foes a fear, to friends a festal robe.
And spread in rhythmic lines the sacred story
    Of freedom's triumph over all the globe.

Stand by the flag, on land, on ocean billow,
    By it your fathers stood, unmoved and true ;
Living, defended; dying, from their pillows,
    With their last blessing, passed it on to you.

Stand by the flag, though death-shot 'round it rattle,
    And underneath its waving folds have met,
In all the dread array of sanguine battle,
    The quivering lance and glistening bayonet.

Stand by the flag, all doubt and treason scorning,
    Believe, with courage firm and faith sublime,
That it will float until the eternal morning
    Pales in its glories all the lights of time.

                              ANONYMOUS.

THE BEAUTIES OF THE AMERICAN FLAG.

I have seen the glories of art and architecture, and mountain and river; I have seen the sun set on Jungfrau, and the full moon rise over Mount Blanc; but the fairest vision on which these eyes ever looked was the flag of my country in a foreign land. Beautiful as a flower to those who love it, terrible as a meteor to those who hate it; it is the symbol of the power and glory and the honor of fifty millions of Americans.

GEORGE F. HOAR, 1877.

[By permission, from "Army H..."]

OUR GRAND OLD FLAG.

Children, see that grand old banner
   That in "sixty-one"
Waved above the walls of Sumter,
   Where the war begun.

    See our flag so grandly waving,
      Emblem of the free!
    Every star and stripe proclaiming
      Land of liberty!

Every stripe records a blessing,
   Every star a state
Of our Union still progressing,
   Free from brother's hate.

Now in peace it smiles upon us
   From its glorious height,
Promising us future vict'ry
   Since our cause is right.

Oh! revere that grand old banner,
   That from "sixty-one,"
Sires so nobly battled under
   'Till the war was done.

                J. P. MARTIN.

A MEMORABLE COMMAND.

"If any one attempts to haul down the American flag, shoot him on the spot."

JOHN A. DIX.

OUR COUNTRY'S FLAG IN SWITZERLAND.

At Geneva, Switzerland, it was pleasant to American eyes, sailing across Lake Leman, on the Fourth of July, to see "Old Glory" floating merrily out. Not one solitary flag, but the buildings far and near flaunted the stars and stripes. One hotel was fairly draped with our banner. "We will follow the flag," said one of our party, and to the Grand Hotel de La Paix we went, and quite a bit of a Fourth of July we had among the Alps. The landlord surprised us on going down to dinner with a magnificent banquet. Waiters, decorated with a rosette of red, white, and blue, ushered us into the hall; bouquets and silk American flags, with every star in its place, enlivened the table, and no sooner were we seated than a concealed band of music struck up our national airs.

OUR BATTLE-FLAGS.

Nothing but flags — but simple flags,
Tattered and torn, hanging in rags;
We walk beneath with careless tread,
Nor think of hosts of mighty dead
Who've trod beneath in days gone by,
With burning cheek and eager eye,
And bathed the folds in life's red tide,
And dying blessed, and blessing died.

Nothing but flags — they're bathed in tears;
They tell of triumphs, hopes, and fears;
Of mother's prayers for boy away,
That he return some coming day.
Silent, they speak, and tears will start;
We see them now with aching heart,
And think of those who're ne'er forgot —
Their flags came home, why come they not?

Nothing but flags — we hold our breath
And view with awe those types of death.
Nothing but flags, yet thoughts will come,
The heart must pray, though lips be dumb!
They're sacred, pure; we see no stain
On those loved flags, come home again;
Baptized in blood, our purest, best,
Tattered and torn, they're now at rest.

MOSES G. OWEN.

THE NATION'S FIRM BULWARK — THE SONS OF VETERANS.

The Sons of Veterans is the most patriotic and unselfish organization on God Almighty's footstool. The proudest title on earth is that of an American citizen. The most unselfish patriot in the world is the Union soldier. He gave his home and life in defense of his country. The proudest inheritance is that of a son whose father wore the blue. The people in the old countries are proud of their blue blood, but the old blue coat our fathers wore is aristocracy enough for us. We would have mankind remember that in rivulets of blood on southern battle-fields our fathers established the proposition that there is room for but one flag in their country, and that is the stars and stripes. Any other flag, whether it be the red rag of anarchy or the stars and bars of the rebellion, must come down. It will be a sad day for this nation when it forgets that the flaunting of the red flag of anarchy by the mob or the waving of the stars and bars over the grave of a rebel chief is damnable treason. So long as the rebel flag is waved from the housetops, so long as the sons of confederate soldiers organize to perpetuate the memories of the war from their point of view, and teach treason to their children, just so long will it be the duty of the sons of Union soldiers to organize for the purpose of perpetuating the glories of the principle for which they fought. The Sons of Veterans are organized to keep green the graves of the veterans, to care for the helpless veterans and their families, and to inculcate the principles of liberty in the minds of the people. We know no North or South, and recognize only loyalty to the flag. As the decimated ranks of the veterans sweep down the western slope we are rushing up the eastern hillside, ready to take the flag from tired hands and preserve it unsullied to the end. We have forty thousand men at present drilled and equipped, who are ready for action at the shortest possible notice, and the other sixty thousand of the one hundred thousand membership will, if danger calls, be only a few hours in securing arms to start for the nation's defense.

CHARLES F. GRIFFIN,

From "The C W orn d Sto .

GOV. YATES AND THE AMERICAN FLAG.

Governor Yates, of Illinois, received a letter from a town in the southern part of the state, in which the writer complained that traitors in his town had cut down the American flag, and asked what ought to be done in the premises. The Governor promptly wrote him as follows:

"Whenever you raise the flag on your own soil or on the public property of the state or country, or at any public celebration, from honest love to that flag and patriotic devotion to the country which it symbolizes, and any traitor dares to lay his unhallowed hand upon it to tear it down, then I say shoot him down as you would a dog, and I will pardon you for the offense."

UNDER THE FLAG OF OUR FATHERS.

Soldiers are we from the mountain and valley,
   Soldiers are we from the hill and the plain;
Under the flag of our fathers we rally;
   Death for its sake is but living again.

We have a history told of our nation,
   We have a name that must never go down;
Heroes achieved it through toil and privation;
   Bear it on bright with its ancient renown!

Who that shall dare say the flag waving o'er us,
   Which floated in glory from Texas to Maine,
Must fall, where our ancestors bore it before us,
   Writes his own fate on the roll of the slain.

Look at it, traitors, and blush to behold it!
   Quail as it flashes its stars in the sun!
Think you a hand in the nation will fold it,
   While there's a hand that can level a gun?

Carry it onward, till victory earn it
   The rights it once owned in the land of the free,
Then in God's name, in our fury we'll turn it
   Full on the treachery over the sea!

Peace shall unite us again and forever,
   Though thousands lie cold in the graves of these wars,
Those who survive them shall never prove, never,
   False to the flag of the stripes and the stars!

                    GEORGE H. BOKER.

From The C W   n S

RALLY 'ROUND OUR FLAG.

Rally 'round the flag, boys —
    Give it to the breeze!
That's the banner we love
    On the land and seas.

Brave hearts are under it,
    Let the traitors brag;
Gallant lads, fire away!
    And fight for the flag.

Their flag is but a rag —
    Ours is the true one;
Up with the stars and stripes!
    Down with the new one.

Let our colors fly, boys —
    Guard them day and night;
For victory is liberty,
    And God will bless the right.

                JAMES T. FIELDS.

HYMN TO THE FLAG.

Hail! peerless flag! o'er our broad land waving,
    O'er every ship man'd by our brave tars ;
Dearer thro' age for past dangers braving,
    Float on undaunted, thou banner of stars.

Oh, lovely flag! the bright sun addressing,
    Smiling, salutes thee daily, his pride ;
Happy the breeze with joyful caressing,
    Adds to thy beauty new graces beside.

Oh, valiant flag! when storms of death rattle,
    Beating thy folds in war's cruel wrath,
Shining amidst thy heroes in battle,
    Visions of glory illumine their path.

Oh, peaceful flag! with blessings attending
    Ever we'll pour our love at thy shrine ;
Warm hearts surrounding, strong arms defending,
    Flag of our fathers! all honor be thine.

                COMRADE E. W. FOSTER.

[From "The United States Flag, a Protest"]

THE TATTERED BANNER.

These banners, soiled with dust and smoke,
   And rent by shot and shell,
That through the serried phalanx broke —
   What terrors could they tell!
What tales of sudden pain and death
   In every cannon's boom!
When e'en the bravest held his breath,
   And waited for his doom.

To bear these colors aloft was a signal for the enemy's bullets, often bringing swift and certain death; but they never trailed in the dust nor lacked a gallant bearer.

ANONYMOUS.

OLD GLORY.

Thank God! the struggle's over, peace reigns in all our land,
United now as brothers forever let us stand;
One flag, one country,—Union—no North, South, East, or
    West,
Each vieing with each other to do the very best;
With millions of defenders to rally at its call,
"Old Glory" is an emblem that truthful speaks to all;
We love to look upon it as it proudly floats on high,
No star is darkly blotted, no stripe but of royal dye.

A. READ WALES.

THE FLAG OF THE SIXTH INDIANA

In 1861, when the Sixth Indiana started to the front they had no flag. The fact becoming known to the patriotic ladies of Louisville, Kentucky, they presented the regiment with a fine one as it passed through their city. When it was worn out the State of Indiana furnished a new one, and the old one was sent back to the Governor for safe keeping. After a lapse of twenty-nine years, upon the occasion of the visit of the survivors of the Sixth Indiana to Louisville as the guests of the Louisville Legion, with which regiment it was brigaded during the war, it was very much desired to take the old flag which was given to them by the Louisville ladies to show it to them and to say, "'*Here's your flag.*' We honored it then and we love it now, though its bright colors are faded and it hangs in tatters; we have brought it to you to-day that we may greet you beneath its sacred folds, point to its scars and crimson stains, and say we tried to do our duty." But when the committee called upon the State Librarian they were informed that it could not be loaned. It is really a pity that upon such an occasion, and for a flag which never belonged to the state, it could not be loaned on the strength of a bond for a few days.

RETURN OF THE FLAGS TO THEIR STATES.

Aye, bring back the banners and fold them in rest!
They have wrought their high missions, their holy behest!
Stained with blood, scorched with flame, hanging tattered and
    torn,
Yet dearer, by far, than when bright they were borne
        By brave hearts to glory!

As we gaze at their tatters, what battle-fields arise,
Fields flashing in deeds of sublimest surprise!
When earth rocked with thunder, the sky glared with fire,
And havoc's red pinion dashed onward in ire!
        Deeds deathless in glory!

Press the stars to the lips, clasp the stripes to the heart!
Let us swear their grand memories shall never depart!
They have waved in this contest of freedom and right,
And our eagle shall waft them, wide streaming in light,
        To our summit of glory!

There — hope darting beacons, starred shrines, shall they glow,
Lighting liberty's way to the breast of the foe;
'Till her spear smites with splendor the gloom, and our sun,
One broad central orb, shall again brighten one
        Mighty nation of glory!
                  ALFRED B. STREET.

By permission, from "Acire Havert ぉ"

OUR BANNER ON THE SOLDIER'S BIER.

Take thy banner! and whene'er
Thou shalt press the soldier's bier,
And the muffled drum shall beat
To the tread of mournful feet;
Then this spangled flag shall be
Martial cloak and shroud for thee,
When our weeping eyes shall see,
Thy tired form in wakeless sleep.

OUR FLAG AND THE SOLDIER'S GRAVE.

Sleep on, brave heart, the flag you bore
    Throughout the land at last doth wave.
Your bold comrades, now the war is o'er,
    Will plant that banner on your grave.

Enfold him in the stripes and stars,
    He will not dim the brightest beam;
His blood will tinge the crimson bars,
    Add richer luster to its gleam.

ANONYMOUS.

From Following Our Fa: _ permission

WRAPT IN OUR FLAG.

Wrap 'round him the banner,
 It cost him his breath,
He loved it in life
 Let it shroud him in death,
Let it silently sweep in its gorgeous folds
 O'er the heart asleep and the lips that are cold.
                          ANONYMOUS.

www.ingramcontent.com/pod-product-compliance
Lightning Source LLC
Chambersburg PA
CBHW021835230426
43669CB00008B/979